VOLUME 3

Miss Brenda's

BEDTIME STORIES

This book is lovingly presented to

_____

By: _____

On this special occasion

_____

Date: _____

Miss Brenda's

BEDTIME STORIES

BRENDA WALSH

Based on
True Character-Building Stories for the Whole Family!

3ABN BOOKS

Three Angels Broadcasting Network
P.O. Box 220, West Frankfort, Illinois
www.3ABN.org

Pacific Press® Publishing Association
Nampa, Idaho
Oshawa, Ontario, Canada
www.pacificpress.com

Design/Layout: Chrystique Neibauer "CQ" I cqgraphicdesign.com
Cover Photography: David B. Sherwin
Project Coordinator: Mellisa Hoffman I finaleditservices.com
All images used under license from Shutterstock.com, unless otherwise noted.

The author assumes full responsibility for the accuracy of all facts and quotations as cited in this book.

Additional copies of this book are available from two locations:

Adventist Book Centers®: Call toll-free 1-800-765-6955 or visit http://www.adventistbookcenter.com.

3ABN: Call (618) 627-4651 or visit http://www.store.3abn.org.

3ABN Books is dedicated to bringing you the best in published materials consistent with the mission of Three Angels Broadcasting Network. Our goal is to uplift Jesus Christ through books, audio, and video materials by our family of 3ABN presenters. Our in-depth Bible study guides, devotionals, biographies, and lifestyle materials promote whole person health and the mending of broken people. For more information, call 618-627-4651 or visit 3ABN's Web site: www.3ABN.org.

Scripture quotations marked NIV are from the HOLY BIBLE, NEW INTERNATIONAL VERSION®. Copyright © 1973, 1978, 1984 by International Bible Society. Used by permission of Zondervan Publishing House. All rights reserved.

Scriptures quoted from NKJV are from The New King James Version, copyright © 1979, 1980, 1982, Thomas Nelson, Inc., Publishers.

Scripture quotations marked NLT are taken from the Holy Bible, New Living Translation, copyright © 1996, 2004, 2007. Used by permission by Tyndale House Publishers, Inc., Wheaton, Illinois 60189. All rights reserved.

Scripture quotations marked KJV are from the King James Version of the Bible.

Library of Congress Cataloging-in-Publication Data:

Walsh, Brenda, 1953-
Miss Brenda's bedtime stories : true character building stories for the whole family! / Brenda Walsh.
    p. cm.
ISBN 13: 978-0-8163-2513-9 (hard cover)
ISBN 10: 0-8163-2513-8 (hard cover)
1. Christian children—Religious life—Anecdotes. 2. Families—Religious life—Anecdotes. I. Title. II. Title: Bedtime stories.
BV4571.3.W35 2011
249—dc22

2011007590

11 12 13 14 15 • 5 4 3 2 1

Linda Johnson, Brenda Walsh, Ken Micheff, Cinda Sanner, Jim Micheff

Brothers and Sisters

When I count my blessings, I always thank God for my precious brothers and sisters who God has allowed me the privilege of growing up with. I can't imagine what life would be like without their love and support. No matter what project God is asking me to do, or what circumstance I am facing, they are right there beside me, encouraging, strengthening, and supporting me every step of the way. They are not only my family, my best friends, my support team, my closest social network, and my prayer partners, but most importantly, my spiritual mentors! I know I can count on them no matter what! They truly are, "the wind beneath my wings!"

We have played together, laughed together, cried together, faced tough times together, and through it all—loved each other! I feel blessed to be a part of the *Micheff family*, where our parents raised us not only to love Jesus and accept Him as our personal Savior, but also to share His love with others. It is an added blessing that in our adult years, God has brought us together to work for Him. All five of us are in full-time ministry!

It is with heartfelt love that I dedicate volume three of *Miss Brenda's Bedtime Stories*, first to my Lord and Savior, and then to my precious sisters and brothers, Linda, Cinda, Jim, and Ken. I love you with all my heart and am looking forward to the day when we will all be gathered together at Jesus' feet!

ACKNOWLEDGMENTS

With Special Thanks

Dr. Kay Kuzma

I want to thank Dr. Kay Kuzma for all her hours and hours spent editing *Miss Brenda's Bedtime Stories*. She is one of the most generous, kind, and talented people I know and these stories would not have been the same without her! I admire and respect her professionalism, creative writing skills, and her loving service for others. Her love for our Lord and Savior shines through in all she does. She has blessed my life in so many ways and I thank God for the gift of her friendship.

Brenda Walsh

Author Appreciation

I want to personally thank each of these best-selling authors for their generous contribution of stories. It is truly an honor and privilege to include them in this book. Each author was personally selected to be a part of *Miss Brenda's Bedtime Stories* because of their creative and professional writing style, incredible talent, and love for Jesus! To each of them, I extend my sincere and heartfelt thanks!

Doug Batchelor

Karen Collum

Kenneth Cox

Jim Gilley

Karen Holford

Linda Johnson

Kay Kuzma

Charles Mills

Seth Pierce

Kay D. Rizzo

Kimberley Tagert-Paul

Jerry D. Thomas

Nancy Van Pelt

ACKNOWLEDGMENTS

With Heartfelt Thanks To . . .

MY STORY AND PHOTO TEAM: *Battle Creek Academy* for opening your doors for the cover photo shoot. *Ted and Bonnie Bloomfield* for the many hours spent developing the Excel spreadsheet. *Mellisa Hoffman* for your project coordination, organizational skills, being the "spelling champ," tenacity to *getting the job done*, and your loyalty and friendship! *Hannah and Lance Hoffman* for your patience during all the long hours your mom spent working on the book project. *Chrystique Neibauer* for the incredible layout and graphic design of the entire project, for extra long hours, patience, and being a friend I can count on! *Lucy Neuharth* for sewing the frog-hat. *Joel Sanner* for frog-hat photos. *Dave Sherwin* for volunteering your time to photograph each cover. *Ina Stanaland* for writing endless e-mails and reading and categorizing all the stories.

MY MINISTRY SUPPORT TEAM: *Carole Derry-Bretsch* for e-mailing your numerous friends to find the perfect photos and, most of all, for being my lifelong friend! *Peg O'Brien Bernhardt* for always being there for me, listening, believing in me, and for your love and friendship! *Kari Avery-Duffy* for hours spent researching stories, answering letters, and your dedication to the Kids' Time ministries. *Marie Macri* for being a precious friend— always there for me. I love you dearly! *Rita Showers* for a lifetime of memories, friendship, and the best neighbor a girl could have! *Nancy Sterling* for mentoring me, looking out for my best interests, and for your loving friendship!

MY FAMILY: My precious husband, *Tim Walsh*, for never complaining about the time I spent working on this project, for your constant support, help, and patience, but most of all, for your unconditional love you give me every day! *Rebecca Lynn and Linda Kay* for your love and support and allowing me to share your stories. My parents, *James and Bernice Micheff,* for your prayers, letting my team take over your house, for endless hours finding photos, and for all those great meals! To my *sisters, brothers, grandsons, aunts, uncles, nieces, and nephews,* for your patience and loving understanding concerning the many hours I spent working on this project, even though you would have preferred I was spending time with you! I am so very grateful for my precious family and love you with all my heart!

Those who shared their stories with me:

Rebecca Coffin	Ron Reese
Trevor Ferrell	Jeff, Kari, and Levi St. Clair
Mary Le Grice	David Stewart
Gail Logan	Bob Willett

3ABN *Kids' Time*

Brenda Walsh is a vivacious, loving, and generous Christian with a heart for ministry and a burning desire to share the love and joy of Jesus. When she started praying, "Lord, use me in a special way," God did! And the resulting amazing miracle stories have been an inspiration to thousands across the world who have heard her dynamic presentations or read her attention-grabbing books. Her message is one of encouragement and hope to those who want to be used by God. Hearing Brenda is truly a life-changing experience, whether it's at a women's ministries retreat, a prayer conference, a church-based weekend event, or a children's ministries seminar.

Miss Brenda & Maxwell

Photo taken by: John Lomacang

Brenda is best known as "Miss Brenda," the producer and host of *Kids' Time,* a popular daily children's program on Three Angels Broadcasting Network (3ABN). She is also a frequent guest on the 3ABN *Today* program, cooking and singing with her sisters, Linda and Cinda. Together they have authored vegan vegetarian cookbooks and recorded several gospel CDs. Brenda also has her own solo CD, *My Wonderful Lord.*

Brenda is the author of *Battered to Blessed,* her life story of being a victim of domestic violence, and *Passionate Prayer,* which features her own personal stories of answered prayer. She has also co-authored several books with her friend Kay Kuzma.

Photo taken by: cqgraphicdesign.com

Photo taken by: cqgraphicdesign.com

In addition to ministering to others, Brenda is a registered nurse, interior decorator, and floral designer. Brenda is married to Tim Walsh, has two grown daughters, Becky and Linda Kay, and two grandsons, Michael James and Jason Patrick.

www.kidstime4jesus.org

LESSON INDEX

TABLE OF CONTENTS

Stories can have power to touch us and change us. They can help us understand what another person is feeling and help us see things from a new perspective. They can help us understand "Why?" and see the reasoning behind "Be careful!" They can help us learn lessons without having to suffer from making mistakes! That's why Jesus taught by telling stories. He knew that stories help us understand.

This book is full of stories told for the same reasons. So much effort, love, and prayer have gone into collecting and preparing *Miss Brenda's Bedtime Stories*! Based on true stories contributed from people around the world, each one has been written especially for Miss Brenda by beloved and best-selling authors (and some written by Miss Brenda herself!). They are sure to be loved by children and treasured by parents and grandparents and all who read them.

Brenda has shared these stories to help kids everywhere develop strong characters, understand important lessons, and most important, learn to be a good friend of Jesus. These pages are full of stories that are heart-touching, soul-searching, fun-filled, adventurous, and meant to be shared!

May these stories bring laughter to the eyes, wisdom to the mind, and understanding to the heart of everyone who hears them. And may there be a double blessing of peace and joy to each grown-up who takes a few precious moments to share them with a child.

Be sure to collect all five volumes of
Miss Brenda's Bedtime Stories!

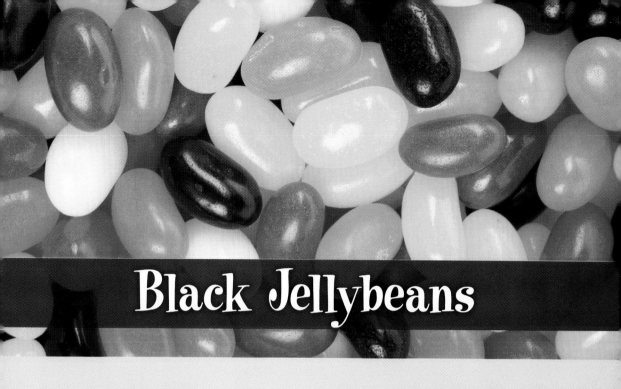

Black Jellybeans

Gail's family was pretty careful about what they ate. Mom baked whole wheat bread and prepared good, healthy soups and casseroles, with not too much cheese, milk, sugar, or salt. As Dad said, "There's nothing better than the good Lord's fruits and vegetables just the way He made them." So desserts and snacks were usually apple wedges, crispy carrots, or raisins and walnuts. But once in a while, on Saturday night, the family would play games together and have a special treat.

Gail's favorite treat was jellybeans. She loved the pinkish-red strawberry ones and rosy-red cherry ones. They were especially good if you ate them with a lemony-yellow one. But her most favorite ones were the licorice-flavored black jellybeans. The rest of the kids knew how much Gail loved them, so they usually ate all the beautiful colored ones—leaving the black jellybeans for Gail.

One Saturday night, after putting the games away, Dad announced, "Time for bed, kids. We've got to get up early tomorrow so you can get your weekend chores done before the church picnic at the park. 'Early to bed . . . early to rise, makes kids healthy, wealthy, and wise!'" The children laughed. Dad was always coming up with his version of some famous saying to emphasize what he wanted them to do. Then he turned to Gail and handed her the bowl of leftover jellybeans. "Gail, would you take the jellybeans to the kitchen and put them in the cupboard, please? And don't eat any more."

She took the bowl Dad handed her and headed toward the kitchen. Just as she was ready to put the jellybeans in the cupboard, she noticed that there were a lot of black jellybeans on the top of the pile! Wow! They looked so good.

She looked around to make sure no one was watching her. She was alone. Since no one was looking, she knew exactly what she was going to do—take a few more black jellybeans.

Gail picked out one black jellybean and shoved it quickly into her mouth. *Ummm!* It was so good that she had to have another. She picked out a couple more and shoved them into her mouth. Then another! Pick and shove. Pick and shove. Soon she couldn't fit anymore jellybeans in her mouth, so she carefully put the bowl in the cupboard and sneaked quietly down the hall to her bedroom with her cheeks bulging. She hoped no one would see her or talk to her because there was no way she could answer with her mouth stuffed so full! When she got to her room she sat down on her bed and chewed and swallowed, chewed and swallowed. Her mouth was so full that it was difficult to swallow. Finally, the last of the black jellybeans went down her throat and she crawled into bed. She knew she should say her prayers, but what would she say? All she could think about were those black jellybeans her dad told her not to eat. They hadn't tasted nearly as good as she had imagined. Over and over in her mind she could hear her dad's voice saying, *"Don't eat any more."* She had not only disobeyed her dad, which made her feel guilty enough, but she had taken something that didn't belong to her. She felt like a thief—and that made her feel even worse.

She picked up a book and started leafing through the pages trying to make herself forget about the jellybeans. But the more she tried, the more her conscience hurt—and the more her stomach began to feel queasy. It felt like all those jellybeans were playing soccer in her tummy. She put down the book and pulled the covers over her head. She turned to one side, then the other. She tried hard to go to sleep. She shut her eyes tight and counted to ten frontwards. Then she counted to ten backwards.  But nothing seemed to work. She just couldn't get comfortable. And all the time the soccer match in her tummy was making her feel worse and worse. She tossed and turned, turned and tossed, and tossed and turned some more.

Finally, she knew what she had to do. She quietly got out of bed, tiptoed down the hall, and slowly opened the door to her parents' room. She felt her way over to her dad's side of the bed.

"Dad," she whispered. "Dad, are you awake?" No answer. "DAD," she called a little louder right into his ear.

Dad woke up with a start and reached out to her. "What's wrong, Gail? Are you OK?"

"No, Dad. I disobeyed you and now I can't get to sleep."

"What do you mean you disobeyed me? What did you do?"

"Dad, after you told me to put the jellybeans away, I picked out the black ones and ate them." With her admission, Gail started to sob as the whole story tumbled out. "I can't go to sleep because I disobeyed you and stole the jellybeans and ate them and now I feel sick."

Dad gave her a big bear hug. "Well, honey," he said, "I think you have learned a good lesson about obedience. I love you and I forgive you. Jesus loves you and He will forgive you too. Let's go back to your room and ask Him right now." So Gail and her dad knelt together by her bed and prayed to Jesus, asking Him to forgive her for disobeying. Gail immediately felt better. Dad tucked her back into bed, gently kissed her forehead, and said, "I'm proud of you, sweetie."

"I love you, Dad," Gail responded as Dad turned out the light.

Now that her conscience was clear, the black jellybean soccer match was over . . . and with a smile on her face she fell fast asleep! ■

> *Confess your sins to each other and pray for each other so that you may be healed.*
> —James 5:16, NLT

Church Monkey

"What would you like to eat?" Mom asked as she and Blake moved through the open-air market in downtown Manila. All around them people were hunting for bargains among the colorful stalls of produce and other items.

"Mangos," Blake answered. "I love mangos."

"Oh, really?" Mom said, smiling at her son. "I thought ice cream was your favorite."

"It is," Blake answered with a smile, "but I was thinking how great a big bowl of ice cream would taste with a juicy mango sliced on top."

Mom laughed as she handed him some coins. "OK. You go see if you can find some mangos, and if not, buy yourself something special. I'll look for some rice and a ripe melon. Meet me at the car in fifteen minutes."

Blake nodded and headed out on his own, weaving through the crowds of people. He reached into his pocket

and felt the pesos his mom had given him. He had enough money for a big bag of yummy mangos. It was fun being a missionary kid living in the Philippines.

A few minutes later, while standing at a stall piled high with mangos and other tropical fruits, Blake suddenly felt as if someone was staring at him. Spinning around, he found himself nose to nose with a baby monkey perched on a wooden stand. Blake looked at the monkey. The monkey looked at Blake. Then a smile began to spread across Blake's face as he read the sign, *Monkey for Sale*. Suddenly, he knew what he wanted even more than mangos.

Mom shook her head when she saw Blake coming toward the car with a monkey perched on his shoulders. "Blake, what have you done?" she exclaimed. "I thought you were going to buy mangos, and instead, you've come back with a monkey! What's your dad going to say?"

Blake thought for a moment as he reached up and took hold of the small hands that were tugging on his ear, and gently pulled the monkey down into his arms. "He'll say, 'Hey, where did you get that cute monkey?' "

Mom laughed in spite of her misgivings as she placed her bags in the back of the car. She studied the charming little creature and sighed, "We've already got chickens and more than enough lizards to keep us entertained. But a monkey!"

Blake grinned. "He won't be any problem. I'll take good care of him. And he was a bargain. Only a few pesos. Dad likes bargains."

When they got home, Mom shook her head again. "Well, let me hold him while you bring in the bags from the car. I suppose you've given him a name?"

"Petey," Blake called over his shoulder.

Mom looked down at the small creature in her arms who was looking up at her with big, wide-open eyes. "Hello, Petey," she said. "You're not going to give us any problems, are you?"

This time, the monkey smiled.

During the weeks that followed, Petey did what baby monkeys do! He grew bigger and bigger. But he also grew to love his family and looked forward to Blake and his two younger brothers playing with him. Once Dad got over the shock of discovering that a little monkey was a part of their family, he built a shelter for him in the branches of a tree right beside the house. Even though Petey was securely tied to the tree, he could climb about freely and even scamper to the ground. It wasn't the jungle, but Petey had been born in captivity, so he didn't know the difference. All he knew was that he loved being the center of attention among the children and the adults living on the mission compound.

Each week, Blake and his family would put on their best clothes and walk to a building at the far end of the road. Petey would watch them from the perch in his tree, cocking his head from one side to the other when he would hear the singing and piano music. He was curious. What did the people do there?

One particular day, as the music began to drift throughout the compound, Petey decided he needed to check out where all the people had gone. After all, he was part of the family and he didn't like being left behind. It was lonely not having anyone to play with.

So, Petey began to wiggle, and squirm, and stretch, and pull, and tug at his rope. He groaned and grimaced, puckered his lips, and squinted his eyes. The rope was the only thing keeping him from discovering the great mystery waiting at the far end of the mission. And as he worked on the rope, it began to fray. Little by little, he pulled on the loose threads and the rope got weaker and weaker. Just a few more tugs and the rope snapped. Petey was free at last! Now, where should he go? He could have run away to the jungle. He could have playfully swung from branch to branch on the tall Narra tree that grew in the middle of the compound. Or he could have opened the screen door that led to the kitchen and made a BIG, BIG mess. But Petey had other ideas as he started loping down the road toward the church.

As Blake sat quietly in the pew listening to a woman read from the Bible, he wasn't thinking about Petey. Instead, he was thinking about how fun it was attending church in a foreign country. He liked worshiping with people who spoke different languages and dressed differently than he was

used to back in the United States.

"Let us kneel for prayer," he heard his father say from behind the pulpit. Everyone leaned forward and dropped reverently to their knees as the piano played softly. Then Dad began to pray.

A moment later, Blake heard a soft commotion behind him. Being a curious boy, he opened his eyes just a little. He gasped in disbelief! There, walking quietly and reverently down the center isle of the church, was Petey, dragging a short length of rope behind him. The monkey's eyes were focused on the pulpit, behind which stood a very familiar man.

Blake nudged his mom and pointed as Petey ambled by. Now it was Mom's turn to gasp! Her eyes grew big and round as she watched the family pet walk toward the front of the church. It was as if he was responding to an altar call of a preacher who had asked the people who wanted to give their lives to Jesus to come forward.

Dad was just getting to the part of his prayer where he was thanking God for His many blessings, when he felt as if someone was staring at him. Opening his eyes just a little, he saw Petey sitting on the edge of the pulpit smiling at him.

Dad was shocked! He quickly grabbed the runaway monkey and tucked him under his suit jacket just as he ended his prayer. But there was a problem. After prayer, Dad was supposed to direct the choir as they sang a soft, prayerful song while the people remained kneeling reverently.

Turning around, he motioned for the pianist to play an introductory chord. As he lifted both arms to signal the choir to start singing, Petey peeked out from Dad's coat and smiled a great big toothy smile at the choir members.

There was a loud gasp from the choir loft. They couldn't believe their eyes—*a monkey in church!*

Only two people were able to sing the song. The rest were trying very hard not to laugh—something that choir members aren't supposed to do when singing a prayer response.

When the song ended, Dad excused himself and walked quickly out the side door.

Later that day, as Dad and Blake sat on the steps of the house watching Petey play among the branches of his tree, Blake commented, "I have a feeling that my friends back home have never seen a monkey in church. What do you think, Dad?"

"I think you're right, Blake. In fact," Dad added, "I doubt if very many people in the Philippines have ever seen a monkey walk down the aisle!"

"Why did Petey come to church, today?" Blake asked. "He's a monkey. He doesn't know what church is."

Dad thought for a moment. "He likes people and music. But most of all, he was curious—and I think he wanted to be with his family. I just wish more people would want to go to church as much as Petey did. Maybe the next time we don't feel like going to church, we should think about Petey and do whatever is necessary to overcome what is holding us back, so we can enjoy worshiping with God's people."

"Petey taught us an important lesson today, didn't he?" Blake commented.

"Yes, he sure did," agreed Dad with a smile. "God created the animals and there are many lessons we can learn from them. Enjoying the animals that live in different parts of the world is one of the blessings of being a missionary."

"I love being a missionary," Blake said. "I can't think of anything in the world that I'd rather be. Besides, where else would you ever find a monkey who goes to church!" ■

Go therefore and make disciples of all the nations ... teaching them to observe all things that I have commanded you.
—Matthew 28:19, 20, NKJV

Cliff Hanger

"Hey Lexi, you daydreaming or what?" called Felicia. "Grab your gear from the truck and let's go!" As members of a rappelling club, they were attending a special training event for beginners. They had participated last year and were returning to advance their skills. That is, Felicia and Miguel were interested in practicing their skills. Lexi was there, however, just to keep them company.

Lexi hurried to catch up with her friends. She took a deep breath. The scent of pine filled the air as they hiked up the trail. She loved looking up through the tree branches toward the blue sky and then down at the granite cliffs beneath. As she gazed at the cliffs, she thought about the terrifying experience she had last year. She shuddered. She would never do that again!

Once on top of the mountain, she watched as both Felicia and Miguel began strapping on harnesses to rappel down the cliff. She walked around to the side of the rock, took her camera out

of her bag, and starting taking some photos of the view from the cliff.

"Smile!" Lexi instructed as she pointed the camera at her friends. She enjoyed taking their pictures, but it just wasn't the same. How she wished she could be going down with them. The three were always doing things together. But fear now gripped her and she refused to even try. Finally, the two made it to the bottom. Lexi then went back to where the instructors were getting kids ready to go down for the first time.

"How does this go on?" called Abby.

Lexi knew how the harness went on so she and another staff member helped her.

"But, what if I can't do it?" whispered Abby to Lexi.

"Sure you can do it," Lexi found herself saying. "An instructor will go down with you."

Abby shook her head. "I don't think I have enough nerve to step back over the edge of the cliff," she responded with a nervous shudder.

"*Awww*, you'll do fine," Lexi assured her.

"You sound so confident." Abby looked wide-eyed as Lexi helped her get her helmet on. "I bet you've done this a hundred times."

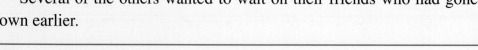

Lexi wasn't sure she should tell Abby about her one and only experience going down this cliff.

"Hey, we've got one extra harness here. Who else wants to go down?" called out an instructor.

Several of the others wanted to wait on their friends who had gone down earlier.

"Will you go down with me?" pleaded Abby.

Just then it was hard to tell whose eyes were the biggest with fear, Abby's or Lexi's.

"Please!" beckoned Abby. "Please go down on the rope beside me."

Before Lexi realized what she was doing, the instructor who had helped Abby put on her rappel harness was helping Lexi into the harness on the rope right next to Abby's.

The nightmare of a year before flashed through Lexi's mind. She, too, had been hesitant about learning how to rappel.

Finally, she was all strapped in and the instructor led her to the edge of the precipice just as Abby was getting ready to rappel a short distance away from her.

"I don't know if I can do this!" Abby called out as she knelt at the edge and contemplated crawling backward over the rock.

"You can do it," encouraged the instructor who was going to rappel with her. But Abby wouldn't budge.

"Come on!" Lexi called out. "We'll do it together!" Then she whispered a prayer, "Oh, dear Jesus, please help Abby and me. We're both so scared! With Your help, I know we can do this. Amen."

She then crawled backward over the edge. This was the part that spooked her the most.

"Are you with me, Abby?" Lexi called out.

Slowly, the younger girl scooted one foot and then the other over the edge. "Ahh! I'm afraid!" she screamed.

"Relax, Abby." Lexi tried to sound calm. "Let's go down together,

OK? Take a deep breath and pull a little rope through your harness like this—just like the instructors showed you."

"Ohh!" squealed Abby. "This is so scary."

"But it's kind of fun, right?" Lexi tried to sound brave. "Now let a little more rope out."

Even though the instructor was right there, Abby followed Lexi's lead.

"Ohh! Ohh! It's so far down!" shrieked Abby.

"Don't look down," cautioned Lexi. "Look up, look at the rock, or look at me."

Together they continued their descent.

"Abby, you can even push off the cliff a little like this," Lexi squatted toward the face of the cliff and thrust her body out a bit.

"Oh no! I couldn't do that," Abby countered, content to merely let more rope out.

"Come on. It's a lot of fun," Lexi heard herself saying. "See, you can even hop a little from side to side when you go down."

Suddenly, memories from the frightening experience a year ago flooded her mind. She had gotten carried away jumping back and forth and had gotten her rope tangled up on a jagged rock. Before she realized what was going on, her body had flipped upside down and her instructors had to free her. It was a nightmare she would never forget and was the reason she had vowed to never rappel again!

Just then Lexi noticed Abby starting to hop out a bit.

"Don't jump around too much," she quickly warned.

Lexi now realized that she herself was hanging over the very spot where her rope had gotten tangled up last year. "Dear Jesus, please help me through this. Help me not to be afraid," she prayed.

"I'm really enjoying this!" shrieked Abby as if she was on a wild ride at an amusement park.

Suddenly, it occurred to Lexi that God had sent Abby into her life to help her get over her own fear. In coaching Abby through the descent, she was also helping herself.

"Oh, this is so much fun!" squealed Abby.

"Yes, it is!" Lexi had to agree.

Before long, the two reached the bottom.

"How's my girl?" beamed a lady who came running up to Abby.

"Oh, Mom, it was wonderful!" Abby looked thrilled. "And this is Lexi. She guided me down the cliff."

"Nice to meet you, Lexi! Thanks for helping my daughter." Abby's mom smiled warmly.

"Oh, it was nothing. I was glad to do it." Lexi blushed and then went in search of Felicia and Miguel.

As she started up the path, she ran into their instructor. "Hey! Have you seen my friends?" Lexi asked.

"Yes, I saw them a few minutes ago. They waited down here for a while, but when you didn't come they went looking for you," Mr. Bernstein replied. "If you want to hike back up, there's a group about to go."

"Thanks, Mr. Bernstein."

"Oh, Lexi, it's great to see you getting back up there and giving it another try." He smiled as he gave her a pat on the shoulder.

Lexi smiled too.

Once on top of the mountain again, Lexi found both of her friends each putting on a harness.

"Going somewhere?" she shouted.

"Lexi, where have you been?" Felicia and Miguel called back.

"Well, never mind about me. Were you two thinking of going down the mountain without me?"

"Lexi?" Miguel looked puzzled. "We thought you told us you would never do this again."

"Yeah, that's what I thought, but God had other plans! Is someone using this other harness?" questioned Lexi.

"No, it's all yours," offered the instructor.

As the three friends descended the cliff together, Lexi told them about her experience that day and how God had given her the courage to conquer her fear. ■

> *I lift up my eyes to the hills—*
> *where does my help come from?*
> *My help comes from the LORD,*
> *the Maker of heaven and earth.*
> *He will not let your foot slip—*
> *he who watches over you will not slumber.*
> —Psalm 121:1–3, NIV

Brownie Goes Berserk

Brownie was a no-nonsense cow. She had a mind of her own and sometimes she could be downright mean. No one messed around with Brownie. Brownie had what you might call an attitude problem, but when it came to producing milk, she made the sweetest, creamiest milk in all of Oklahoma—at least that's what Ken thought. *Ummm,* was it good!

Brownie had been the family's milk cow for almost as long as Ken could remember. Milking her had always been his older brother Donald's job. But now that he had left home for boarding school, Ken was the lucky boy who had to get up before breakfast and milk her. And then, he would milk her again every evening before supper. Milking the cow was just one of the chores a kid was expected to do when he lived on a small farm—regardless of whether he liked it or not.

It didn't take Ken long to discover that as long as Brownie was munching sweet, green alfalfa, she was a contented cow. So as soon as her nose went down into the hay, Ken would grab his three-legged stool and put it next to her hind leg. It had to be close enough so she wouldn't kick Ken and far enough away so she wouldn't step on him. The milk bucket had to be placed in just the right spot too, so Brownie wouldn't put her foot in it or kick it over. But the thing Ken hated most about milking was Brownie's tail—especially when prickly cockleburs got stuck in it. Her tail was just the right height so when she swished it to shoo away the flies, if Ken happened to be in the way, it would hit him smack in the head. *Ouch! That hurt!*

Roscoe the family dog was Ken's constant companion, especially at milking time. Roscoe loved licking up any spilled milk and would sit patiently beside Ken as he worked, hoping for a taste.

One spring morning, just as the sun was coming up over the horizon, Ken got dressed and headed out with Roscoe to the barn to milk Brownie. But Brownie was not waiting at the barn door as she usually was. Where was she? Ken rarely had to go looking for her. Maybe a fence was down and Brownie had wandered away. Or maybe wild animals had attacked her and she was hurt.

"Dad! Dad!" Ken raced to the house. "Dad, Brownie's not at the barn," he shouted.

"She may have had her calf last night," Dad replied. "You better hurry and find her. But be careful. When she has a baby, she gets very protective!" he added. "Come get me if she's had her calf and I'll help you get her up to the barn."

Ken knew exactly what Dad meant. When Brownie had a calf, she was downright mean. And if he happened to get too close when she was in one of her mean streaks, look out! Ken was small for his age and to him, when Brownie was angry, she was an enormous monster! If he happened to come upon Brownie when she was in a foul mood, there was no telling what she might do to him. But Dad had asked him to go and find her. *Hopefully,* he thought, *I'll be able to see whether or not Brownie has had a baby, without her seeing me. And if she does see me, I sure hope I'll be close enough to a tree so I can climb it and get out of the way of her sharp horns.*

The pasture was large. Where should he start looking for Brownie? *Jesus, help me to know where to find her,* he prayed. Ken saw their small herd of beef cattle grazing off to one side of the pasture. Brownie wasn't with them. He thought, *Where would Brownie go to have a baby?* He looked around. *Probably she'd go into the woods where there would be some protection for her newborn.* He began to walk toward the woods.

It wasn't long before he spotted her, and by her side was a newborn calf. He only got a quick glance however, for at that very second, Brownie turned around and saw him. She began to shake and lower her head. Next, she began pawing the ground. Ken knew what was coming next. Brownie was going to charge him. He had thought through this possibility and his plan had been to climb a tree. But Brownie was between him and the trees. He had only one choice. He would have to make a run for it across the pasture to the barn—and right now it seemed as if it were a hundred miles away. Hopefully, he could make it before Brownie trampled him.

Ken took off running for dear life. His feet pounded the ground. He didn't take time to look back, but he could hear Brownie's thundering hooves getting closer and closer. He knew she was gaining on him. Never had he run so fast and prayed so hard. *Dear Jesus, please help me reach the safety of the barn!*

Suddenly, he realized he was never going to make it. Brownie was so close he could feel her hot breath on his neck. This time, Ken cried out, "Jesus, help me!"

And at that very moment, Roscoe came running around the corner of the barn, barking wildly. This distracted Brownie just long enough for Ken

to reach out and grab the barn door. He jumped inside and slammed the door behind him, just as Brownie's horns crashed into the door with an awful thud!

Ken was shaking so violently, he collapsed onto the hay and lay there panting. Roscoe wiggled through a hole in the barn wall and started licking his face. On the other side of the barn door, they heard Brownie give a few snorts, then turn around and trot back to her baby.

After making sure that Brownie was nowhere around, Ken cautiously opened the barn door and made a beeline to the safety of the house. Ken was still shaking as he told Dad about being chased by Brownie.

Dad put his arm around Ken and said, "I'm glad you're safe, son. God puts natural feelings of love into the hearts of animal mothers to care for and protect their young—just like your mom and I love and protect you. We'll give Brownie a little time to settle down and be with her baby, and then we'll go down together and bring them back to the barn where you can milk Brownie, and her calf will be safe." A few minutes later, as they bowed their heads around the breakfast table, Ken thanked Jesus for sending Roscoe at just the right time to distract Brownie and allow him to get safely to the barn.

Later that day, Ken watched his dad confidently walk up to Brownie, give her a couple pats, pick up her calf in his arms, and shoo her ahead of him toward the barn. Ken kept his distance just in case Brownie decided to charge him again, but Brownie never even looked in his direction. When they got to the barn, Ken filled the manger with hay. Then, while Brownie munched her fill, he milked her. This time the bucket got even less milk—for not only had the calf gotten its fill, but Roscoe got an extra bowl of warm milk as Ken's way of saying *Thank you*. ■

> *The LORD will keep you from all harm—*
> *he will watch over your life.*
> —Psalm 121:7, NIV

Nervous Nellie

Nellie was shy—very shy—especially at school. She just didn't feel she measured up to the other kids. Besides, she was afraid that someone would make fun of her if she made a mistake. Even though she got good grades, she thought she wasn't as smart or as talented as the rest of the kids in her class.

One morning, she was so scared of embarrassing herself by missing a word in the spelling test that her stomach began churning. She begged to stay home, but Mom knew she just had *spelling-bee butterflies* that would go away as soon as her test was over. As Nellie left her house to walk to school, she was so nervous that she almost threw up her breakfast.

Then there was the day that her teacher announced there would be a math test on fractions right after recess. Nellie froze with fright. She was having trouble understanding the last math worksheet and hadn't yet had time to ask her parents for help. She was scared

to ask her teacher because she thought Mrs. Burns would think she was dumb. She broke out in a cold sweat thinking she would flunk the test. *I know,* she said to herself. *I'll ask Heather to help me.* The two friends worked together all recess until Nellie felt confident she could pass the test.

There were a couple of kids in class who were outstanding artists and Nellie felt they could draw far better than she. The art teacher was trying to teach them to draw with perspective—with the objects in the front of their picture larger than the ones in back—just like things looked in photographs. Nellie loved art. She drew all the time, but she had a difficult time accepting her own work—and she was afraid others wouldn't either.

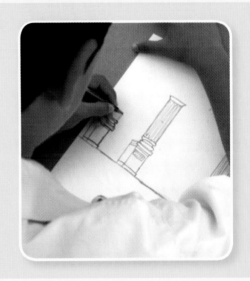

"If only I could draw like you," Nellie sighed as she passed Jed's desk. "That building looks so real."

"My dad's an architect and he taught me to use a ruler and slant the lines so it looks like the front part of the building is big and the back is smaller and farther away," Jed replied. "Let's see your picture."

"No, it's not as good," Nellie said as she held her picture behind her back.

"What do you mean?" Jed asked as he pulled it away from her.

Nellie rolled her eyes. "I'm not good at art."

"What are you talking about?" Jed exclaimed. "Your picture is as good as mine—it's just different!" But nothing her classmates could say could convince Nellie that what she did was *good enough.*

Then, at the beginning of the new term, Nellie nearly fainted when Mrs. Burns announced, "Starting today, I want each of you to take turns standing up and reading out loud in front of the entire class. This will help you to become more confident whenever you give a speech."

Everyone looked stunned. They were used to reading in small groups, but not in front of everyone!

Mrs. Burns continued, "Turn to page thirty-seven in your reading book."

A knot formed in Nellie's stomach. *Please help me, Jesus,* Nellie prayed. *I can't do this. No way!* She tried to slide down in her desk so she wouldn't be so visible.

"Nellie!" Mrs. Burns suddenly called, "Would you please begin reading paragraph one under the title, 'The Prancing Pony'?"

Nellie glanced at her friend Heather. She didn't look any more excited about this than Nellie did.

"Where?" Nellie asked in a shaky voice. She was so scared, she didn't even hear the instructions.

Mrs. Burns immediately realized just how afraid Nellie was. "I know it's scary to read in front of the whole class, Nellie. The other kids are thinking how lucky they are that I chose you and not them." The kids giggled nervously.

"I chose you because I'm confident you can do this. You're a good reader. Remember, doing something the first time is always scary. But the more you do it, the more confident you will become." There was a pause, and then Mrs. Burns added, "And who cares if you make a mistake? We all make mistakes. That's one of the best ways to learn."

As Nellie stood, the redness crawled up her neck and covered her face. *How can anyone possibly read in front of a classroom full of kids, especially smart ones?*

"Start with the first paragraph on page thirty-seven, right under the title, 'The Prancing Pony,' " Mrs. Burns repeated.

Heather looked at Nellie and shrugged her shoulders, but there was nothing she could do. Nellie didn't have the faintest idea how to get out of this. She tried not to look at the other kids who, if she messed up, she was sure would be shaking with laughter. Instead, she forced herself to keep looking straight at the paragraph. She had read lots of books to herself. She loved to read, just not out loud—and certainly not in front of the entire class. She quickly read the paragraph.

"Thank you, Nellie," said Mrs. Burns. "You did a good job. Now Jed, would you read the next paragraph?"

Jed stood up, took a deep breath, and started reading, "There . . . there is no . . ." His hands were shaking as much or more than Nellie's shook. Then, BOOM! Jed's reading book hit the floor.

Everyone laughed. Mrs. Burns was not pleased. "Children, children, please, this is not funny. It's easy to drop a book when you're scared. I know you were laughing at the book falling, but to Jed it feels like you're laughing at him. I think you need to apologize."

"Sorry. Sorry. Sorry." Soft apologetic whispers arose from around the room as everyone buried their heads in their books.

Jed quickly picked up his book from the floor and sat down.

"Heather, why don't you read the next paragraph for us?"

Heather began reading, "There is no . . ." and continued to read the entire paragraph with ease. She didn't stumble through her words. She didn't appear to be the least bit nervous or scared like Nellie.

After school, as Nellie climbed the steps to her home, her mind was racing and her spirits were low. Why did she have to be so shy? Why did she always have to feel like she wasn't as good as the other kids? She got good grades in spelling, math, art, and reading. But the other kids just made it look so easy. *Why do I have to study so hard?* she thought.

The next day during reading class, Mrs. Burns didn't call on Nellie first. Instead, she started at the first desk in the first row and went on down the line, not skipping or bouncing around.

Please, Jesus, help me, Nellie thought. *Please don't let me make a fool of myself!* Then, just as Mrs. Burns asked Nellie to take her turn, the bell rang.

"You lucked out," Heather said to Nellie as they headed out to recess.

"Wait until tomorrow," replied Nellie darkly. "She'll probably start with me for sure. I'll make a fool of myself in front of everyone."

"You don't know that," said Heather reasonably. "You love to read. Just relax and it will be OK. I get scared, too, when it's my turn to read out loud."

"You do?" asked Nellie. She was more than a little surprised. "I thought I was the only girl who got nervous."

"No, I think most of us are scared," said Heather reassuringly. "Nobody wants to be laughed at or made fun of. Nobody!"

"Thanks, Heather," Nellie said. "It's nice to know that I'm not the only one who's afraid."

The next day, Mrs. Burns started at the first desk in the last row and again went down the line, asking the students to read.

Nellie quickly counted out the paragraphs and figured out that she would have to read paragraph number nine. She quickly read it over and over again making sure she knew every word. *Please, Jesus, help me,* Nellie prayed. *Help me not to mess up!*

"Nellie," Mrs. Burns called her name.

When Nellie stood up, she felt like Jesus was right there with her. Her grip on the book was firm. She looked around the room and then fixed her eyes on the paragraph. Nellie read in a clear voice, "There, lying in some tall weeds, he found the shovel and the sack of jars. He was amazed. He wondered if the shovel and sack might have rolled down the hill . . ." When she finished, she realized she wasn't as nervous and her voice didn't shake at all!

"Very good, Nellie," Mrs. Burns said. "Jed, you may read the next paragraph." He looked at Nellie before he began and smiled. He, too, looked more confident.

After Jed finished, Mrs. Burns complimented him and said, "You know, kids, God has given each of you special talents. Some of you are better in math, some in art, or P.E., or reading. But the most important thing is that you appreciate each other's talents while at the same time you accept and develop your own. I'm proud of each one of you for being willing to try. You can always be confident that Jesus will help you to do your best, if you just ask Him." ■

Thus says the LORD to you: "Do not be afraid nor dismayed because of this great multitude, for the battle is not yours, but God's."
—2 Chronicles 20:15, NKJV

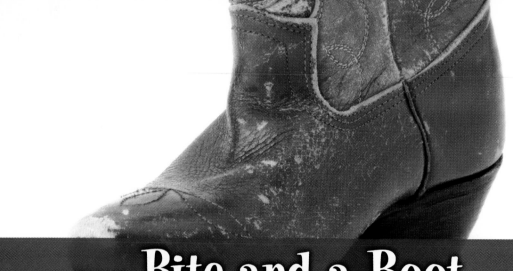

Bite and a Boot

Allen was a great kid at school, but at home he had a very bad habit. He loved to tease his little sister, Mindy. He knew it was wrong. He had memorized the golden rule: *Treat others as you want them to treat you*. He certainly didn't like it when others teased him, but for some reason, he enjoyed hearing Mindy squeal in distress. So when he got bored and couldn't think of something more exciting to do, Allen would come up with a way to torment her. He knew exactly how to "get her goat," as their grandmother always said.

One time, he took Mindy's shoes just before the school bus arrived so she missed the bus. Sometimes at night, he hid under her bed and grabbed her ankles as she climbed in just to hear her scream. Once, he put a rubber snake under her pillow; another time, he chopped off her favorite doll's long, beautiful curls. That prank backfired as his parents made him spend his allowance to pay for a new doll. Even

though Allen had been embarrassed carrying the doll up to the checkout counter, he still didn't learn his lesson. In fact, no matter what his parents did to stop the teasing, nothing seemed to work. That's the way it is with bad habits. Unless you really want to change, it just doesn't happen.

One day, during recess, Allen's friends, Josh and Conner, were bragging about all the things they could do. Allen, not wanting to be outdone, boasted, "I can make my little sister cry anytime I want to, without even touching her."

"Ah, no you can't." Conner shook his head in disbelief. He had three sisters of his own and there was no way he had that kind of control over them.

"Ya wanna bet?" Allen countered.

"*Hmmph!* I'd like to see you do it." Josh was curious.

"Fine." Allen tilted his nose in the air. "Come home with me after school today, and I'll prove it to you."

Instead of listening as Mr. Andrews explained long division in math class, Allen concocted his plan. He knew that whatever he did it would have to be dramatic to impress his doubting friends. By the time the closing bell rang, he knew exactly what he would do. His conscience bothered him a little, but he managed to push it out of his mind by thinking of how impressed his friends would be.

"So, what are you going to do?" Josh asked as he fell in step with Allen outside the schoolyard.

"Yeah, what are you going to do?" Conner chimed in as he slung his backpack over his shoulder.

"You'll see." Allen confidently led his friends up the walk and into the house. The door had barely slammed behind them when Josh challenged,

"Where's your little sister? Let's see if you can make her cry."

"*Shhh,* I don't want Mom to hear us. Don't worry! I'll show ya. Just watch!"

Allen called to his sister in his sweetest voice. "Mindy, where are you? What are you doing?"

"I'm in the family room playing with my dolls," Mindy replied.

"Where's Mom?" Allen looked around for his mother as he led Josh and Conner through the house and into the family room. Scattered across the floor were stacks of miniature clothing for Mindy's collection of dolls, along with a doll house full of furniture and a pink sports car.

"Hi." Mindy looked up at her big brother and his two friends.

Allen anxiously glanced down the hallway and up the stairs. "Where's Mom?"

"In the kitchen, fixing supper."

"Perfect," Allen muttered under his breath as he cast a knowing grin toward Conner and Josh. "Mindy, ya wanna play a game with us?"

Mindy, always eager to be included in her older brother's activities, hopped up from the floor, her dolls temporarily abandoned. "Sure. What are we going to play? Tag? Hide-and-seek?"

And that's when Allen sprang his mean surprise on Mindy. He lifted his own arm to his mouth and chomped down on it just above his wrist. Immediately, deep, crimson teeth marks left an imprint on his arm. Taking a quick breath from the sudden pain, Allen let out a wail and ran to the kitchen, yelling and sobbing dramatically. "Mom! Look . . ." he whimpered, holding his wrist up for his mother to see. "Look what Mindy did to me!"

Mindy, eyes wide in disbelief, ran after her brother. Confused and frightened, she skidded to a stop at the kitchen doorway while Josh and Conner cowered in the hallway beyond the dining room.

"Mindy!" Mom exclaimed as she examined the curved teeth marks indenting Allen's wrist. Mindy knew that biting was absolutely against house rules, and Mom's punishment would be swift. "Young lady! You go upstairs to your room!"

"But Mom, I didn't . . ." Tears sprang into her eyes.

"Now!" Mom pointed toward the stairs. "We'll discuss this later!"

"But I didn't do it! I didn't do it! I didn't!" Tears streamed down Mindy's angry face as she stomped up the stairs. "Nobody ever listens to me! It's just not fair!"

Glancing over her shoulder, she spotted a giant grin on her brother's face. Behind him, Conner and Josh

stared in amazement as if trying to decide whether to run home or stay to see what would happen next.

At the top of the stairs, Mindy's gaze landed on a pair of Allen's cowboy boots which had thick, wooden heels. Without thinking, she grabbed one of the boots and flung it wildly down the stairs. "You're mean!" she wailed.

Still grinning over his victory, Allen watched the boot spin in the air toward his head, like a missile headed for its target. Not having time to duck, the wooden heel hit him with a loud thud, right between his eyes.

Everything went black. Allen dropped to the floor. A few minutes later, Allen felt a throbbing pain on his forehead where the boot hit. When he opened his eyes, he didn't feel much like grinning. He was surprised to find himself stretched out on the floor at the base of the stairs with his worried mother and sobbing sister leaning over him. Nearby, he saw the white faces of his two friends hovering behind them.

"I didn't mean to hit you, Allen! Honest! I didn't mean to hit you!"

Mindy wailed, gently patting her brother's shoulder.

He winced and groaned when his mother lifted his head onto her lap. "He's going to be OK, Mindy. See! He's coming to already." Mom brushed a lock of Allen's brown hair off his forehead. "Mindy, go to the freezer and get a bag of frozen peas."

"Peas?"

"Yes, peas. And hurry! The cold will help take away the pain and stop the swelling."

Mindy quickly ran from the room and returned with a bag of frozen peas. Allen winced when Mom placed the bag on his forehead.

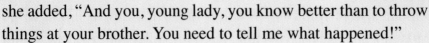

"There," she said, "keep this on your head."

Mom turned to Josh and Conner. "You two had better go home. I don't think Allen will feel much like playing today." And to Mindy, she added, "And you, young lady, you know better than to throw things at your brother. You need to tell me what happened!"

Between sobs, Mindy told her mother the whole story, including her brother's lie about her biting him, and how she was so frustrated she threw his cowboy boot down the stairs.

"Is this true?" Mom asked.

"Well, yes, I guess so." Allen's cheeks reddened.

"Yeah, Mrs. Drake. It's true," confided Josh as he picked up his backpack.

"But it's partly our fault too," added Conner. "We were all bragging and Allen boasted that he could get his sister to cry without touching her. We didn't believe him, so he was proving it to us."

A bewildered frown came across Mom's face. "Kids, I want you to learn something from this. Bad habits get you into trouble. And teasing is a very bad habit."

Still dizzy from the injury, Allen said, "I think I've learned my lesson this time. No more teasing—and no more bragging. Mom, please forgive me."

Then he turned to his sister, "Mindy, I shouldn't have made Mom think you were mean and a liar too. I'm so sorry."

Allen recovered from his head wound, but he would always remember the lesson he learned that day. Between his punishment for teasing and the bump on his head, Allen would never forget the day he traded his little sister . . . *a bite for a boot!* ∎

The Lord detests lying lips, but he delights in men [boys and girls] who are truthful.
—Proverbs 12:22, NIV

Angel in the Berry Patch

It was haying season on the farm where Cole lived with his older brother and sister, Kyle and Elizabeth, and that meant exhausting days out in the field. Cole didn't mind going to bed early, but it was sometimes hard to get up with the sun. Breakfast was over and it wasn't even 7:00 A.M. yet!

Dad laid his spoon down beside his plate, wiped his mouth with his napkin, and opened the family Bible to his favorite verse, Psalm 91:11, "For He shall give His angels charge over you, to keep you in all your ways." Then, as was the family's custom, they joined hands around the table and bowed their heads as Dad began to pray, "Lord, watch over Mom as she does her household chores and watch over us as we work in the fields, especially when we're around the tractors. Amen."

Cole liked being old enough to run the tractors on the farm. Perched on a tractor seat, he felt like he could see the entire world. Out in the barnyard,

Dad reviewed the safety rules for operating the tractors, including what to do if the tractor should begin to roll. Cole yawned and wiped the sleep from his eyes. He had heard the same speech every morning for weeks.

"Mom needs to do the books while I work on old Bessie, here." Dad patted the back tire of the first tractor he and Mom had purchased after they bought the farm. "OK!" Dad's grin stretched from ear to ear. "Go team! Get out there and bale some hay!"

How can Dad be so cheerful so early in the morning? Cole wondered as he trailed after his sister and brother to the barn where they greased every fitting on the tractors, bailer, and rake. Dad always said if you take good care of the farm equipment it would last longer.

Then Kyle, Elizabeth, and Cole climbed onto their appointed tractors and headed down the highway. Being the oldest, Kyle led the way. As it was Cole's first year doing farm work, he went second, and Elizabeth brought up the rear.

The surface of the water glistened in the sunlight as Cole's tractor rolled past the duck pond. He filled his lungs with the sweet aroma of the morning dew and smiled. *It's going to be a good day,* he decided. *It would be nice if the temperature would stay as cool as this.* Cole drove the four miles down the highway where he followed Kyle onto a dirt and gravel farm road. The road curved and descended to a ten-acre field they had cut and tedded a couple of days earlier. Tedding hay involved using the rake in a different position and fluffing the grass to help it dry quicker before bailing and storing it in the barn.

Running the tractor and bailer had been fun at first, but now, after so many days of hard work, Cole wasn't so sure. Elizabeth jockeyed her tractor into the lead position, shifted the gears, and began raking the field. Cole and Kyle followed on their tractors, baling the hay. At the end of

the last row, Cole watched as Kyle drove his tractor around the corner of the field and up the hill toward a second field filled with scrubby trees, stumps, and blackberry bushes.

That's when it happened! Cole turned the steering wheel to make the corner, but he didn't notice how close he was to the edge of the gravel road. The rear tractor tires began to slide toward the ditch. Desperate to correct his mistake, Cole cranked the steering wheel toward the bank on the opposite side of the road.

"Help me, Jesus!" he cried as the tractor shot down the bank and barreled through the blackberry bushes. Terrified, Cole clung to the wheel with all his might as the tractor bounced across the rough hillside. He seemed helpless to steer. First, the wheel yanked to the right, then the left, then back to the right as he tried desperately to stop.

To Cole, it seemed like forever before the tractor came to an abrupt halt in the middle of a giant patch of blackberry bushes. His heart pounded and his body quivered as he hopped off the idling tractor. Blood oozed from the scrapes and scratches on his arms, legs, and face made by the sharp blackberry thorns. Slowly and painfully, Cole inched his way through the tangle of thorns, branches, and roots and into the clearing by the road. Up the hill, Cole saw his older brother and sister looking frantically for him.

"Cole!" Kyle shouted as he and Elizabeth ran to meet him. "What happened? Where did you go? I looked back and you had disappeared!"

"Oh, Cole, are you OK?" Elizabeth looked at her brother's cuts and scratches. "We were so worried. We didn't know what happened to you."

"I'm OK," Cole said in a shaky voice. "Just scared and all scratched up." Cole fought back his tears as he tried to explain, "When I turned the

corner, my rear tires began to slide into the ditch. The next thing I knew I was bouncing through stumps and blackberry bushes. When the tractor stopped, all I could see were the blackberry bushes—everywhere!"

"So where did you leave the tractor and the bailer?" Kyle asked.

"Come on, I'll show you." Cole took his sister and brother to where he had abandoned the tractor.

They stared in disbelief at the jagged path the tractor and bailer made through the blackberry bushes. Cole had barely missed several tree stumps on both sides of the path. If Cole had hit a stump, it would have flipped the tractor onto its side, and Cole could have been seriously hurt.

"Whoa!" Kyle gasped. "How did you do that?"

"I . . . I . . . I don't know. There was no way I could steer. First it yanked to one side, then to the other. So I just held on to the steering wheel and prayed for Jesus to help me!" Cole admitted.

"I'm so glad you're all right," Kyle said with a quivering voice.

After Kyle slowly made his way through the blackberry bushes, he climbed on the runaway tractor and slowly inched it back into the clearing.

"Did I hurt the tractor or the bailer?" Cole asked.

Kyle eyed the tractor from outside the blackberry patch. "I don't think so. But that's not what's important. I'm just thankful you didn't get seriously hurt."

The tractor engine purred, as if waiting to go back to work. "When I didn't see you behind me, I got scared and prayed too," Kyle admitted. "If the tractor had hit one of those stumps, you could have been killed. Your guardian angel must have held your hands on the wheel to steer you safely through the maze of stumps."

That night at worship, the entire family thanked Jesus for the tractor-riding angel in the berry patch. ■

> *For He shall give His angels charge over you,*
> *to keep you in all your ways.*
> —Psalm 91:11, NKJV

Missing Papers

More than anything else in the entire world, Becky liked being with her friends. She especially loved playing dolls with her best friend, Gena, or tag with the neighborhood kids. The only problem was that Becky's parents had a rule that she must finish her homework before she could play.

One afternoon, Becky sat at the dining room table trying to figure out the answers to a page full of math problems when the phone rang. It was Gena.

"Becky," Gena began, "guess what! I have a new Barbie—you know, the one with the princess dress and tiara. Can you come over and play?"

Becky groaned. She had only done one row of the math problems. That left five more rows to do. "I can't. I still have to finish my homework."

"Oh," Gena sighed, "that's too bad."

"Wait!" Becky shot a quick glance toward the kitchen where her mother

Becky Walsh and her best friend Gena Macri

was preparing supper for the family. "I can do it later."

"Great! My mom said she can pick you up in a few minutes."

"I'll be ready." Becky scooped up her school books and dashed up the stairs, calling as she ran, "Mom, I'm going over to Gena's. I'll be home in time to set the table for supper." The last thing Becky wanted was for her mother to ask if she had finished her homework.

Photos provided by: Brenda Walsh

Once in her room, Becky changed into her play clothes. As she grabbed her Barbie travel case, she cast one last glance at her discarded schoolbooks on the bed. *Hmmm,* she thought, *if Mom sees my unfinished math page* . . . Without considering the consequences, she quickly stuck the homework on the floor in the back of her closet and left for Gena's house.

An hour and a half later, as the girls dressed and redressed their Barbie dolls, Becky spotted the clock on Gena's dresser. "Oh, it's five-thirty. I've got to go home. I promised Mom I'd set the table."

After dinner was over and the dishes were loaded in the dishwasher, Becky remembered her homework and started for her room to finish it, that is, until her mother announced, "Let's go to the mall. I need to purchase a sweater for Aunt Cinda's birthday and your sister needs a new pair of shoes."

The next day, when Becky sat down to do her homework, her neighborhood friends called, "Hey, Becky, do you mind if we come over for a game of tag?"

Becky glanced at her math book and then at the laundry room where her mother was ironing. She thought of her unfinished homework from yesterday. Mrs. Adams hadn't asked her for it. Becky decided she could do two pages of math before going to bed that night. "Sure, come on over."

Becky shouted to her mother as she bounded out the back door. "Hey, Mom, I'll be playing in the backyard with my friends." The door slammed behind her as Becky hurried outside before her mom could reply.

Each day, Becky found it easier to add her unfinished homework to the growing stack of papers in her closet. Then one evening, two months before the end of the school term, Becky came home from playing at Gena's house, and Mom met her at the door. By the frown on her mother's face, Becky knew she was in trouble.

"Hi, Mom," Becky chirped, trying not to sound nervous.

"I just got off the phone from talking with your teacher."

"Oh?" Becky felt a sinking feeling in her stomach.

Mother folded her arms across her chest and tapped one foot on the tile floor. "Mrs. Adams told me that you will have to repeat fifth grade next year."

"What?" Stunned, Becky stared at her mother. "Does that mean all my friends will graduate to sixth grade, and I'll be stuck in fifth with all the babies? How can she do that to me?"

Photos provided by: Brenda Walsh

Becky Walsh

Disappointment flashed across Mom's face. Becky wasn't used to seeing her mother so upset. "She didn't do it to you, Becky. You did it to yourself!"

"No! Why? How?" Becky stammered.

"You haven't turned in any math homework since Christmas. You've been lying, making Dad and me think you had done your math assignments before going out to play. Did you think we wouldn't find out?" The lecture continued, "Why didn't you do your homework? And what did you do with it?"

"It's in the back of my closet under some clothes," Becky stammered.

"Go and get it!" Mom ordered. She waited at the base of the stairs while Becky dashed up to her room for the thick stack of homework papers, ran back down the stairs, and handed everything to her mother. Mom shook her head sadly. "We trusted you, Becky."

Tears ran down Becky's cheeks. "I'm so sorry." She hadn't considered that hiding her homework was lying. And she had really intended to do all her assignments later—but later never came.

"Mom, I'm so sorry. I'll do anything to graduate with my friends. Can't you do something? Please, talk to my teacher."

Mother's lips tightened. "We'll talk with Mrs. Adams tonight at our parent-teacher conference to see what can be done."

That evening, Becky waited nervously on a bench in the hall outside her classroom while her parents and Mrs. Adams discussed the problem.

Photo taken by: cagraphicdesign.com

An hour later, they called Becky into the room.

"Becky," her teacher began, "your parents told me what happened and why you haven't been turning in your homework. We've discussed the situation, and I've decided that if you can do every one of your math assignments between now and the end of school, I'll let you pass."

Becky gasped, "Surely you don't mean every assignment?"

"I do, indeed! Every assignment! No exceptions." And with the teacher's pronouncement ringing in her ears, a solemn Becky returned home with her parents. As Dad eased the car into the garage, he turned to his daughter. "I counted the stack of papers and figured out how many you have to do each day in order to get them done before the end of the school year. You'll also have to keep up with all your new assignments. You are going to be a very busy girl."

Over the next two months, Becky had no time to play with her friends after school. Even on Saturday nights, while her friends were having fun, she was doing homework. Dad and Mom made sure Becky kept to the schedule. Many times her fingers cramped and her head ached, but she knew better than to complain to Mrs. Adams or her parents.

On the last day of school, Becky proudly handed her final homework assignment to Mrs. Adams. Her teacher gave her a big smile and said, "Welcome to sixth grade!" ■

> *Be sure your sin will find you out.*
> —Numbers 32:23, KJV

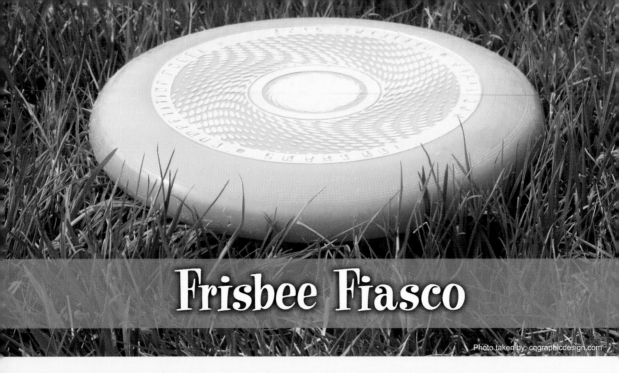

Frisbee Fiasco

"Nathan, settle down!" Grandma warned.

The ten-year-old boy always got very excited when he found someone new to play with. Sometimes too excited.

On this occasion, Nathan was throwing a frisbee back and forth with a boy who lived next door to the church. Normally, Grandma wouldn't care, but the boys were laughing, screaming, and running around like wild animals right next to the church where a meeting was being held.

A gentle nudge in Nathan's heart told him he should listen to his grandma and calm down. Yet, he had so much energy after sitting still in church all morning that all he wanted to do was run, jump, and throw the frisbee.

Nathan knew he should obey his grandma, but he was just having too much fun. Nathan waited until Grandma had gone back inside, looked around to make sure no one else was watching, and then started throwing the frisbee again.

Nathan and parents, Karen and Pastor Doug, and brother, Stephen

Nathan's father was the pastor of the church and was leading out in the meeting. Nathan's mom was at another church meeting across town. And Grandma was busy bringing in food for the guests. That meant that Nathan had a lot of freedom.

The more he played, the more wild and excited he became. He was having a great time running around the church property throwing the frisbee. But that little voice inside kept reminding Nathan that he should obey Grandma.

"Catch!" Charlie shouted as he flung the frisbee to Nathan. But this time, it sailed way over Nathan's head—even over the six-foot chain link fence. Nathan could have walked around the fence, but he wanted to impress his new friend. So instead, he leaped up onto the fence and began to climb over it. That's when it happened.

Just as Nathan was coming down on the other side, his pants snagged on the fence. This made him lose his grip and he began to fall headfirst. He put out his hands to catch himself and when he slammed into the ground, he heard a sickening *snap* and felt a terrible pain in his right wrist.

Nervously, he examined his wrist as he slowly rose to his feet. Horrified, he discovered it was no longer straight, but was now bent in the shape of an *S*. Nathan picked up the frisbee with his left hand and clumsily threw it back to Charlie. He carefully cradled his broken wrist and slowly walked around the fence into the church yard. Humiliated and near tears, he said Goodbye to Charlie and went looking for his grandma.

When Grandma finally brought Nathan to Dad, tears were streaming down his cheeks as he sobbed in pain. His dad quickly examined his arm and shook his head. "We'll need to get you to the hospital right away, son," he said.

The constant, throbbing pain in Nathan's arm was excruciating, but what made it feel even worse was knowing that he had disobeyed Grandma.

Nathan was scared as his father drove him to the hospital. He stared at the *S*-shaped bend in his wrist. *Will the doctor have to cut open my arm to fix the broken bone? Will my arm ever be the same? What if I can never throw again?* As his dad drove, Nathan prayed, *Jesus, please forgive me for not listening to Grandma. And please fix my wrist.*

When they arrived at the hospital, they found the emergency room was filled with hurting people. A nurse told Dad that they would have to wait a while to be seen by the doctor.

Nathan looked around the busy waiting room. It smelled like rubbing alcohol and disinfectant. All the people seemed so sad. Some were constantly sneezing and coughing, while others were covering cuts with bloodstained bandages. A tired-looking man with a green oxygen mask over his mouth was struggling to breathe. Nathan suddenly realized that all he had been thinking about was himself. He had no idea there were so many hurting people.

Nathan looked down at his throbbing wrist and thought about how Jesus was always helping sick people. If his broken wrist had happened in Jesus' day, he would have probably been waiting in the crowd for Jesus to heal him, rather than sitting in an emergency room.

Then he thought, *Jesus must really be sad to see all these hurting people*. Nathan began silently praying, *Lord, please help them. And if there is something I can do to help someone else, please show me*. Nathan's crooked wrist still hurt, yet as long as he was thinking about others, he didn't notice it so much.

Soon, a nurse came over and gave Nathan a little plastic cup with some thick, pink medicine to drink. "This will help with the pain until the doctor can see you," she explained. "He will straighten out your wrist while you're sleeping and put on a cast. You'll have to wear it for a few weeks, but your wrist should be just fine." Nathan felt much better after hearing that.

Just then, the emergency room door swung open and a worried mother rushed in with her daughter. The pretty, young girl looked very scared. She was crying and holding her right arm. Nathan was totally shocked at what he saw—the girl's right wrist was also bent into an *S* shape, just like his! After the mom talked to the nurse, she and her daughter sat down to wait with everyone else. The little girl stared at her arm and whimpered.

Nathan's dad leaned over and suggested that Nathan go talk with the girl to see if he could cheer her up. The pink medicine was starting to work and his wrist was feeling a lot better. Nathan got up and walked over to the girl who was holding her arm tightly.

"Did you break your wrist too?" he asked. The girl looked at Nathan and nodded through her tears. He wanted to be a good witness for Jesus, so he tried to encourage her.

"What's your name?" Nathan asked.

"Susan," she answered softly.

"How old are you?" he asked.

"Nine," she said a little louder.

"Well, I'm ten," Nathan added happily. He then laughed a little and said, "I fell off a fence! What happened to you?" Susan explained that she had fallen while running really fast. He smiled once again and commented, "Oh, you'll be OK. They'll give you some pink medicine that tastes like cherries. Then the doctor will fix your arm while you're sleeping. You'll have to wear a cast for a few weeks, but you can get your friends to sign it. That's what I'm going to do."

By this time, Susan had stopped crying. She even managed a little smile. Amazingly, even the people around Susan and Nathan started smiling as they saw the two kids with broken wrists comparing their injuries.

It wasn't long before Nathan's mom got word about the accident and came to the hospital. She gave Nathan a big hug. Then the nurse called his name, "Nathan Batchelor." He said Goodbye to Susan and he and his parents followed the nurse.

The doctor took an X-ray of Nathan's wrist and gave him a shot that stung just a little. Soon, he got drowsy and drifted off to sleep.

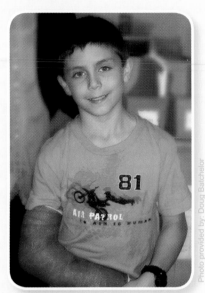

Nathan Batchelor with his blue cast

When Nathan woke up, he had a hard, blue cast on his right arm. He was glad the nurse gave him some special medicine so his wrist wouldn't hurt.

Several days later, sitting at the dinner table, Nathan was proudly showing his family all the signatures on his cast.

"You sure have a lot of friends, Nathan," Mom commented.

"I know! My whole class signed it, even my teacher."

"You are a very fortunate boy to have so many friends. You're even more fortunate that this injury wasn't a lot worse. Your guardian angel must have gone over that fence with you to keep you from falling on your head. You could have been paralyzed for life," Mom said.

"Tell me, what did you learn from this experience?" Dad asked.

"Well, for one thing, it doesn't pay to show off. I should have walked around the fence to get that frisbee."

"Yes, that's one lesson," Dad replied. "Anything else?"

Nathan thoughtfully considered his dad's question as he took a big bite of Mom's homemade bread.

"Well, I guess I learned that it's always good to think of others. When I helped Susan, it made me forget about how much my own arm hurt."

"Those are good lessons, son. But there's also another lesson that I hope you learned. There's a reason God said in the Bible, 'Children, obey your parents.'"

Nathan nodded his head and laughed, then added, "And your grandma too!" ■

Children, obey your parents in the Lord,
for this is right.
—Ephesians 6:1, NKJV

Competitive Carla

You name it, whether it was a computer game, on the race track, or playing four-square during recess, Carla was out to win. She had a competitive spirit that sometimes drove her to feel that winning was more important than enjoying the game or even being kind to her classmates.

"Carla, winning isn't everything," her mom would say when Carla would come home complaining that she had come in second—or worse yet—last!

"I can't help it, Mom. I want to be first. I want to get the highest grade. I want to be the best!"

"Well, sweetie, just remember that winning isn't always about being first. It's being the best person you can be. It's doing what Jesus would do. It's helping others to feel good about themselves. It's important to do your best, but if you happen to lose, just think how happy you're making someone else by giving them a chance to win—and be happy for them!"

"Oh, Mom. You don't understand! The only way to win is to be first." Nothing Mom said changed Carla's mind.

"Well, just don't let your competitive spirit get you into trouble," Mom warned.

Carla shook her head. She had heard this lecture before—and it just didn't make sense. That is until the day that she and her best friend, Emma, were playing four-square during recess.

Four-square was everyone's favorite game at Shelby Middle School.

There were lots of big squares painted on the asphalt playground. Each square was divided into four smaller squares with a 1, 2, 3, or 4 painted in each one. The game started with four players, each standing in one of the small squares. The person standing in square number 4 would begin each round by serving the ball into another player's square. The round continued until one of the players was able to bounce the ball into another player's square in a way that caused that person to miss the ball. When they missed, they were out, and the rest of the players would advance to the next highest position, with a new player coming in at the number 1 position. The object of the game was to get to the number 4 square and the person who could stay there the longest was the winner.

Carla had finally made it to square number 4. She served the ball, and waited for it to be hit back to her. Suddenly, back it came. She stretched to reach it, but it sailed right past her.

"Oops, I missed!" she moaned. She was angry at herself for such a silly mistake and kicked the ball toward the other players. Then she went to the end of the line to wait for another chance to play—and hopefully win.

Emma stepped into the number 4 square and served the ball. Carla watched as Emma put out classmate after classmate. Emma held her winning position for the rest of the recess period, so Carla didn't get

another chance to play. She was frustrated—and just a little jealous with all the attention that Emma was getting, so when the bell rang announcing the end of recess, Carla ran up to Emma and shouted, "Beat you to the drinking fountain!"

Emma took off so quickly though, that Carla didn't have a chance.

"I beat you," Emma called as she bent down to get a drink.

"You're all wet!" laughed Carla as she playfully shoved Emma's head down into the water.

Emma screamed and yanked her head up. Her hand covered her mouth and a scared look was on her face. "You broke my tooth on the fountain!" she cried as she headed into the girls' bathroom.

Carla was right behind her. The mirror confirmed their worst fears. The corner of Emma's front tooth had been broken off and her lip was bleeding.

"Emma, I'm so sorry," Carla wailed. "I was just playing around. I didn't mean to hurt you."

"I know," said Emma as she covered up her bleeding mouth and headed to the nurse's office.

Carla went back to her classroom. The day dragged by. Carla felt horrible. She didn't mean to break Emma's tooth. It was an accident. *If only* she hadn't raced Emma to the drinking fountain. *If only* she could be happy when others won! *If only* she hadn't tried to get back at Emma by pushing her head down into the water! No matter how hard she tried, she couldn't quit thinking about what she had done.

What would her mom say? *If I wasn't so competitive this never would have happened. Mom warned me it would get me into trouble.*

When Carla got home, instead of going inside, she went to the backyard and sat in the swing that hung from the big tree. Should she tell her parents what had happened? She was afraid her mom would say, *I told you so!* And she knew there would be consequences.

Then Carla thought of another one of her mom's lectures: *"If you tell the truth and own up to what you did, there may be a consequence, but if you lie, you'll be in double-trouble!"* Slowly, Carla got up from the swing, picked up her backpack, and opened the backdoor.

"Hi, sweetie," her mom called. "How was school today?"

"Fine," Carla called back hesitantly.

"You don't sound so good. Is everything OK?" Mom asked.

Think, Carla, she said to herself. *What should I do?* In one ear she heard a voice say, *Tell your mom what you did.* In the other, she heard, *You didn't mean to do it. Chances are no one will find out. Forget about it!*

Mom interrupted her thoughts, "Are you OK, Carla?"

"No," Carla blurted out. "I'm not OK! I did something terrible today at school." A tear slipped down her cheek.

"Do you want to tell me about it?"

"Oh, Mom. You were right. I'm too competitive! I wanted to win so much that when Emma beat me at four-square, I was jealous, so I told her I could beat her to the drinking fountain. When she got to there first, to get back at her, I pushed her head down into the water and . . . Mom," Carla sobbed, "I made her chip her front tooth. And her lip got cut—and blood was running all over. It was terrible."

Mom put her arm around Carla and together they walked into the kitchen and sat down at the table. "I already knew what happened, Carla. Emma's mom called me at work. They've already been to the dentist and had the tooth repaired, but it cost a lot of money."

"What about her lip?" Carla asked.

"It will heal. It doesn't look like she'll need stitches."

"Oh, Mom. I'm so sorry. I didn't mean to do it. Instead of being happy for Emma, I was jealous! And look what happened!"

"I know it was an accident," Mom said sympathetically, "but your mistake did cost Emma's family a lot of money. You were just fortunate the dentist was able to fix her tooth. Why don't you spend some quiet time thinking about what you've learned from this experience? And maybe you could ask Jesus to give you an idea about what you should do to help pay for the damage."

Carla went to her room and flopped down on her bed. "Dear Jesus, forgive me for hurting Emma," she prayed. "Please help me to stop being so competitive. I want to be more like You. Please help me find a way to pay for Emma's tooth. I love You, Jesus. Amen."

When Carla finished praying, she got an idea. She quickly went over to the little heart-shaped box where she kept her allowance money. Carla had been saving for horseback riding lessons, but now that would have to wait. She started counting out the dollar bills. Although it wasn't enough to pay the entire dentist bill, it was a start. In addition, she decided she would do odd jobs in the neighborhood until there was enough to pay it all back.

As she handed the money to her mom, Carla announced with a big smile on her face, "Mom, I've learned my lesson. I've asked Jesus to help me remember that the best way to win is to be kind. I'm not going to be *Competitive Carla* anymore!" ∎

Be kindly affectionate to one another with brotherly love, in honor giving preference to one another.
—Romans 12:10, NKJV

Frog-Hat Prayer

Photo taken by: cqgraphicdesign.com

"**H**i," Micah said to a lady standing behind him in the checkout lane of the supermarket, "do you love Jesus?"

"Yes, I do," the lady replied.

"Me too!" Micah said. "I just wanted to make sure, because I know He loves you!"

The lady smiled. "We all need to be reminded, don't we?"

Micah nodded his head. "I'm glad Jesus loves me."

Micah loved to tell people about Jesus. He may have been shy in some situations, but he was never shy about sharing Jesus. In fact, the neighbors called him the missionary boy.

One night, Micah sat at the supper table pushing the peas around on his plate. "Shouldn't some of your supper be going into your stomach, Micah?" his dad asked.

Micah shrugged. "I'm not really hungry."

Mom got a worried look on her

face. "Not hungry? But you're always hungry! Are you sick?"

Micah shrugged again. "I don't know. My stomach hurts."

Dad reached over and put his hand on Micah's forehead. "*Hmmm,* you do feel a little warm. Why don't you go lie down for a little while and see if that helps?"

Micah went to his room and lay down on his bed, but the pain didn't go away. When Mom came in to check on him, Micah was holding his stomach and groaning in pain. "Is it getting worse?" Mom asked. Micah nodded and wiped away the tears. He didn't want to cry, but it really, really hurt.

Mom patted his arm. "I can't leave because I need to take care of your sisters, but I think Dad better take you to the emergency room and have you checked out by a doctor."

Micah's eyes opened wide. "Emergency room! I'm not that sick, am I?"

"You never know," Dad said as he entered the room. "When you're in pain, it means something's wrong—and the sooner we can get help, the better. The emergency room is the only place we can see a doctor at night."

By the time Micah and Dad reached the hospital, Micah was doubled over in pain and could hardly walk. The nurse had Micah lie down on a gurney, took his temperature, and asked lots of questions.

The doctor poked her head around the corner. "Let me know when you have his IV started," she instructed. Tears started rolling down Micah's cheek as the nurse stuck a needle in his arm. He was scared.

"I'm sorry that hurt, but now we can give you some pain medicine," the nurse explained. "See, I just put the medicine in the IV tubing and it drains right into your vein."

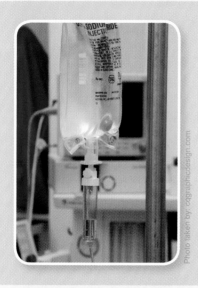

By the time the doctor came to examine Micah, the pain was almost gone.

"Hi! I'm Dr. Ellis. How are you feeling now?" She listened to his heart and his breathing through a stethoscope.

"I feel OK," Micah said. "I think I'm ready to go home."

Dr. Ellis laughed. "I'm not so sure about that," she said. "But it's good to know that the medicine is working." She then pushed on Micah's stomach. He winced a little. Then she pushed on a place right beside his stomach. "Ouch!" he screamed. "That hurts!"

"That's what I was afraid of," the doctor said. "Your appendix is swollen and tender. We need to do a few more tests to make sure, but my guess is we need to take it out as soon as possible."

"You mean surgery?" Micah asked. Micah's dad looked worried. That made Micah even more afraid.

"Don't worry, Micah," Dr. Ellis said. "You won't feel a thing! Your dad can stay with you before and after the surgery. And before you know it, you'll be home again."

After Dad made a quick call to Mom telling her what was happening and asking her to pray, a man in blue scrubs came and pushed Micah's gurney down a long hallway to the elevators, while his dad walked beside him. "I didn't know beds could go in elevators," Micah commented.

"They can in hospitals," the man

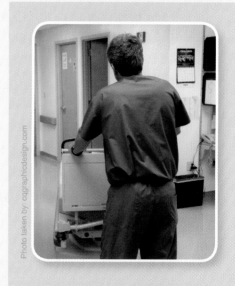

laughed as he parked the gurney in his room. "Your doctor will come and talk to you before your surgery. It shouldn't be too long. Good luck! You'll be just fine!"

After a few minutes, Micah asked, "Dad, what happens when they take out your appendix? Will it take a long time?"

"Let's ask Dr. Ellis to explain it to us," he said as he held Micah's hand.

When Dr. Ellis came in a few minutes later, Micah asked his question. "OK, Micah," she said, pulling a chair over by his bed. "When it's time for surgery, they will push your bed down the hall to the surgery center. Your dad can come along with you. I'll meet you there and when you're ready, we'll give you some medicine that puts you to sleep just like that." She snapped her fingers.

"When you're completely asleep, I'll make a little cut here," she said, pointing to his stomach, "and take out the bad appendix. Then I'll sew it up again. And all this time your dad will be in a waiting room nearby."

Micah squeezed his dad's hand. "Will it hurt?" he asked quietly.

Dr. Ellis smiled. "You won't feel a thing. In fact, you won't know anything until you wake up and the surgery is over."

"Well," Micah said, "that doesn't sound too bad."

Dad then said a short prayer and kissed Micah on the forehead. "Mom's on her way, son. She'll be here when you wake up."

A few minutes later, Micah's bed was rolling down a long hallway to the pediatric operating room. The doors opened automatically to let them through. When they stopped inside the last door, a doctor wearing a green hat with frogs on it met him.

"Hi, I'm Dr. Hixon. I'm the doctor who will give you some medicine to make you sleep and

will stay right with you while Dr. Ellis takes out your appendix. Are you ready?" he asked.

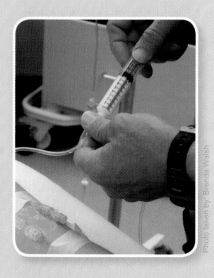

Micah nodded and Dr. Hixon motioned for the nurse to put the medicine in the needle that was in Micah's arm.

Suddenly, Micah said, "Stop! Wait a minute!"

"You don't have to be afraid," Dr. Hixon said.

"I'm not afraid. But I need to ask you a question," he said, looking up at Dr. Hixon.

"What do you want to know?" Dr. Hixon was quite sure that Micah was concerned about what was about to happen to him.

Micah looked straight into Dr. Hixon's eyes. "Do you love Jesus?" he asked.

Dr. Hixon was surprised. He had never had anyone ask him that question before. "Well," he stammered, "I'm not really sure." Feeling a little embarrassed, he quickly changed the subject. The rest of the surgical team, including Dr. Ellis, gathered around. "We need to get started," Dr. Hixon said.

"Excuse me," Micah interrupted, "but do you mind if I say a prayer first?"

"Well, I . . . I . . . guess not," Dr. Hixon said. Dr. Ellis nodded her head in agreement.

"Can everyone please bow your heads and close your eyes?" Micah instructed. Then he began to pray, "Dear Jesus, please be with the frog-hat doctor. I can't remember his name, but You know who he is.

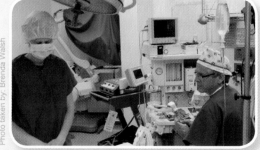

He doesn't believe in You. Please come into his heart and help him to know how much You love him. And help all the other doctors and nurses here to know how much You love them too. In Jesus' name. Amen."

By the end of Micah's prayer, there wasn't a dry eye in the room. "OK," said Micah, "now you can give me the sleeping medicine."

It wasn't long before Mom joined Dad in the waiting room. When the surgery was over Dr. Ellis came in to update them.

"The surgery went very well. His appendix was quite inflamed and, had we waited any longer, it could have ruptured. He's in recovery now. You can sit with him there if you like."

"Thank you so much, Doctor. We've been praying for you."

"Speaking of prayer, I think you should know that Micah said a prayer of his own today in the operating room. We all fully expected him to pray for himself, but he never once asked God to be with him in surgery. He only prayed for each one of the nurses and doctors, specifically that we would know how much Jesus loved us! It was the most unselfish prayer I've ever heard. It made quite an impact on Dr. Hixon, our anesthesiologist. You see, he doesn't believe in God, but after surgery, he asked me if I would take some time to tell him about my beliefs. He knows that I'm a Christian."

Dad and Mom wiped the tears from their eyes. "That's our boy," Dad said. "He's always looking for ways to witness for Jesus!"

When Micah opened his eyes, he saw his parents standing by his bed. They were smiling. "When is Dr. Ellis going to do the surgery?" Micah asked in a groggy voice.

"It's all over," Mom said, beaming. "You're all fixed up!"

Wow, Micah thought, *I don't remember anything!*

Just then, Dr. Hixon came into the room. He ruffled Micah's hair and said to him, "You did great!" Then he turned to Micah's parents. "You sure do have a fine son. Your boy taught me a big lesson today when he prayed for everyone but himself. I've never really been a church-going man . . ." Dr. Hixon stopped for a moment to clear his throat and compose himself, then continued, "Well, I guess what I'm trying to say is, now I have a desire to learn more about Micah's God."

As he turned to leave, he winked at Micah and said, "Hey, kid, I want you to know I'll never forget your frog-hat prayer." ■

Now may the Lord direct your hearts into the love of God.
—2 Thessalonians 3:5, NKJV

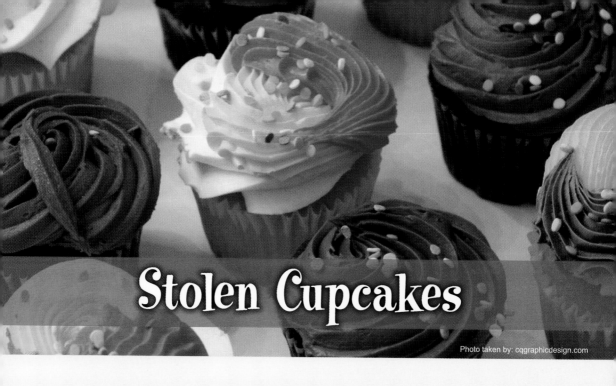

Stolen Cupcakes

"**Y**ou'll never guess what I have in my lunch box," Samantha announced to her friends.

"Frog legs!" snickered Jimmy.

"Yuck!" gagged Dylan. Everyone laughed.

"No, silly," Samantha rolled her eyes. "I've got the best cupcakes in the world!"

Linda, overhearing the conversation, rushed over to take a look as Samantha slowly and dramatically opened her lunch box and took out two store-bought cupcakes topped with creamy pink, yellow, and green frosting, and covered with candy sprinkles. She held them up for all to see.

"I can hardly wait for lunch," Samantha confessed. "My mouth is watering already."

Just then the bell rang. Samantha quickly put the prized cupcakes back into her lunch box, zipped it shut, and

Photo taken by: cagraphicdesign.com

put it on the shelf. Then everyone rushed to their seats to get ready for worship.

During worship, all Linda could think about was Samantha's cupcakes. Her family didn't eat many sweets and they were too poor to buy store-bought cupcakes, especially fancy ones like those! Once in a while, her mom made applesauce or banana cupcakes, but never topped with thick, creamy frosting and candy sprinkles. She wondered what they tasted like. Suddenly, she realized that worship was over. She had no idea what the story was about—and she hadn't even heard the prayer.

Linda tried to get the thought of those cupcakes out of her head. But it was no use. She daydreamed about them in Bible class and even drew pictures of them on the margins of her math worksheet. Finally, it was recess time and everyone hurried outside.

Linda stopped by the restroom and took her time washing her hands. When she came out, she was the only one left in the classroom. She hurried to put on her coat. Just as she started to rush outside, a voice inside her said, *Remember the cupcakes? Wouldn't you like to have a closer look?*

She was curious. *It wouldn't hurt to look at them again, would it?* As she started to reach for Samantha's lunch box, she heard another voice say, *Go ask Samantha.*

But, she thought, *I'm just going to look.* She hesitated. Then the first voice said, *It won't hurt to just open Samantha's lunch box and pick one up.*

She looked around and slowly opened the lunch box and took one out. Suddenly, the good voice inside her said, *It's wrong to touch other people's things—and it could lead to stealing. Put the cupcake back.*

But I'm not going to steal the cupcake, Linda argued with herself. *I'm just going to look at it.* As she held the cupcake, she heard noises outside the door and jumped with fear. *What if the teacher catches me? What if Samantha comes in?*

She was just about to put the cupcake back, when the bad voice spoke again, *Wouldn't you like to know what the cupcake tastes like? Just take a little bite. Chances are Samantha won't even notice if you smooth over the frosting.*

Linda looked toward the door and hurriedly unwrapped a cupcake. She had never stolen anything in her life and didn't want to now, but once again, the bad voice urged her on, *Remember, they are the best cupcakes in the world. What does it matter if you take one bite?*

The good voice immediately countered, *You should ask Samantha first.* But, thought Linda, *Samantha's out on the playground.*

Linda couldn't stand the temptation any longer. She quickly shoved the cupcake into her mouth and took a big bite. The good voice said, *Shut the lunch box quickly and run and tell Samantha.*

Then the bad voice reminded her, *You've eaten so much of the cupcake already, there is no way to hide what you've done, so you might as well finish the cupcake . . . and while you're at it, eat the second one too.*

And that's exactly what Linda did. She stuffed the cupcakes into her mouth and swallowed them so fast that she didn't even know what they tasted like. Then she quickly zipped up the lunch box and put it back where she found it. She was still chewing when she raced to the restroom. She didn't want anyone to catch her. As she washed her face, she looked in the mirror. What she saw was a very sad and scared girl looking back at her. And she imagined the devil gloating, *Ha ha, I gotcha!*

English class was a blur. All she could hear was a voice telling her that now she was a thief and was going to be in big trouble. Tears formed in her eyes. As she wiped them away, she wished she could just run out of the room and disappear. But that would cause too much attention. And where would she go?

At last, Miss Benson announced, "Lunch time. Go wash your hands and get your lunch boxes. Then we'll have prayer."

Linda washed her hands, grabbed her lunch box, and sat quietly in her seat. At last everyone was ready. After prayer, the kids opened their lunch boxes and began to eat. Everyone, except Linda. She wasn't hungry and her cupcake-filled stomach was churning. She glanced over at Samantha who was smiling as she started to open her lunch box.

All of a sudden, Samantha screamed. Everyone looked at her. Everyone, but Linda. Miss Benson and several other students went over to her desk. "What's wrong?" they asked.

Samantha was so upset she was beginning to sob. "Look," she said as she pointed to the inside of her lunch box. "All that's left of my yummy,

delicious cupcakes are the wrappers! Someone ate them!"

Quickly, Miss Benson turned around and looked at the class. The only one who wasn't looking at Samantha was Linda, who had her head down on her desk.

"Linda," asked Miss Benson, "do you know anything about the cupcakes?"

Linda slowly raised her head and shook it. "No," she mumbled and put her head back on the desk.

Miss Benson looked long and hard at Linda and then went back to comforting Samantha. Then she told all the kids to go back to their desks and finish their lunches.

The afternoon hours dragged by. At last, the final bell rang and Linda was the first one out the door. She didn't want to face anyone. Her heart and her legs felt like heavy weights as she walked the short distance home.

Stolen Cupcakes

As she started up the front steps, the door opened. There stood her mother.

"Linda," she questioned, "did anything happen at school today that you would like to tell me about?"

"No, not really," she replied without even looking up.

"Linda," Mom said firmly, "There's something I need to talk to you about. Come sit over here on the sofa." Linda's shoulders slumped. "I heard someone stole Samantha's cupcakes. Was that you?"

Linda looked down at her shoes and stammered, "N-n-no."

"Look me in the eyes and tell me again, did you eat Samantha's cupcakes?"

That was too much for Linda. Suddenly, tears came streaming down her cheeks and the whole story came tumbling out. "Oh, Mom, I'm so sorry. There were two voices inside me. One kept pushing me to take the cupcakes, and the other told me I shouldn't. I guess I listened to the wrong voice."

"That's exactly what happened to Eve in the Garden of Eden," Mom reminded Linda. "God said, 'Don't eat from the tree of knowledge of good and evil,' and Satan said, 'Go ahead, Eve, it won't hurt you.' And you know what happened when Eve listened to Satan! There's always a consequence when you disobey God. Since all your class knows that someone ate Samantha's cupcakes, you need to tell them it was you. Then you're going to have to earn the money to buy Samantha exactly the same kind of cupcakes to replace what you took."

The next day, Linda's feet dragged as lunch time grew near. She didn't know that her mom had called Miss Benson and told her that Linda wanted to say something to the whole class. As everyone opened their lunch boxes, Miss Benson came over to Linda's desk and asked, "Linda, do you have something you want to say to the class?"

Linda stood, shaking with fear. Miss Benson put an arm around her and

MBBS3—6

they went over to Samantha's desk. In a small voice she said, "Samantha, I ate your cupcakes. I'm so very, very sorry. I'll buy you new ones, I promise." By this time tears were running down her cheeks.

Samantha was shocked, "Linda, if you'd only asked, I'd have given you one!"

Linda turned away. As she did, she saw her mom standing in the hallway and rushed out of the room and into her arms.

For the next couple of weeks, Linda worked hard to earn enough money to buy Samantha the store-bought cupcakes. And when she handed them to Samantha, she was reminded that the only voice to listen to was the voice of Jesus. Never again did she want to hear the devil say, *I gotcha!* ■

Photo taken by: cqgraphicdesign.com

> *You shall not steal, nor deal falsely,*
> *nor lie to one another.*
> —Leviticus 19:11, NKJV

Code-Blue Night

It was December 8, 1983. Trevor was eleven years old and watching the local news on television. "The temperature is dropping to an unseasonable low, making this a 'code-blue' night, which means that volunteer vehicles are picking up street people and taking them to shelters. Those people will be the fortunate ones. The man who finds himself sleeping on the streets of Philadelphia tonight will be in danger of freezing to death if he doesn't have a warm blanket or sleeping bag. And now, for the latest sports report . . ."

"Dad, the reporter on television says there's some man in Philadelphia who may be sleeping on the street tonight."

"Yes, Trevor, there are lots of street people in Philadelphia."

"But, Dad, it's a 'code-blue' night."

"So . . ."

"So, that means it's going to be really, really cold."

"So . . ."

"So, if he doesn't have a blanket, he

---

could probably freeze to death."

"I certainly hope that doesn't happen," his dad said sympathetically.

"Dad, we can't let him freeze to death."

"Well, hopefully all the homeless will get to shelters."

"How can we be sure?"

"Trevor, that's not our responsibility," his dad said firmly. "Now let me watch the sports report."

Trevor went back to his room, but he couldn't get the thought out of  his mind. What if somebody was trying to sleep on a cold sidewalk and didn't even have a blanket? He looked at his bed. *I have three blankets on my bed,* he thought. *I don't need them all.* He knew if he were cold, he could just set the thermostat a little higher and the furnace would produce more heat. But the homeless person . . . he couldn't let him die. He *had* to do something. He returned to where his dad was watching TV.

"Dad, I have an extra blanket on my bed."

"So . . ."

"I could give it to someone who's sleeping on the street so he won't freeze to death."

"Trevor, there are hundreds of street people. There are organizations that take care of the homeless. Besides, one blanket won't make that much difference."

"But it would to one person, wouldn't it, Dad?"

"Well, I guess so."

"Then, Dad, please take me downtown to where the street people are so I can give my blanket to someone."

Dad picked up the remote, flipped off the TV, and looked at Trevor. "Are you sure you want to do this?"

"Yes, Dad, I do. I'll go get my blanket!" shouted Trevor as he ran back to his room, grabbed the blanket from his bed, and then stood waiting for his dad at the front door.

Reluctantly, Dad got up out of his recliner, opened the closet, and started to put on his heavy, winter jacket. "Better get your woolen cap and gloves, Trevor. It's beastly cold out there."

It didn't take long to drive to Center City. The family seldom visited this area of town, but Dad knew this was where they would likely find the homeless. Because the night was so dark, it was difficult to see, but Trevor kept his eyes glued to the window, looking for someone who was trying to sleep without a blanket. He couldn't believe what he saw! He had thought there was one homeless man down on the street that needed a blanket. Now he realized that there were many homeless, hungry, and cold men, women, and children.

"There!" Trevor shouted as he pointed to a man lying down outside a building on a grate with a little steam coming out of it. "There's a man who doesn't have a blanket."

Dad stopped. Trevor grabbed his blanket, opened the van door, and walked over to the man. "Hi," Trevor said. "Do you need a blanket?"

The man rose up on his elbow to see Trevor better. "Why, yes," he said. "I could use a blanket. It's mighty cold tonight."

"Here," said Trevor as he handed the man his blanket. "I had an extra one on my bed, and I thought you might need it."

The man looked shocked, but gratefully accepted Trevor's gift.

"Thanks, kid," he said.

"You're welcome," Trevor responded, then quickly walked back to the van.

Before he jumped in and slammed the door, he heard the man shout, "Thank you! Thank you!"

That night, as Trevor crawled into his comfy bed and pulled the blankets up around his chin, the scene that he had just witnessed in Center City played over and over in his mind.

The next morning around the breakfast table, Trevor couldn't keep quiet. He told his mom, brother, and two sisters all about the adventure he and Dad had the night before. "And you won't believe all the people who don't have any place to live!"

Trevor's enthusiasm was contagious. "We've got to do something," the rest of the family agreed.

The next night, the other kids wanted to see for themselves what Trevor was talking about. So when Trevor decided to take the extra pillow on his bed down to Center City to give away to another street person, they went along.

"I bet the people are hungry as well as cold," Mom suggested. "I have a feeling most of them didn't have much, if anything, to eat today—or at least not anything hot."

"Yeah, I bet they didn't either," the kids agreed.

"Why don't we fix them sandwiches and something hot—like soup or a hot drink and bring it down tomorrow night?"

"Great idea!"

And that's how it started. Soon, Trevor and his family were making nightly trips to feed the homeless. At first, it was just a few people, but within days the number grew to over one hundred.

Trevor discovered that helping others had its own reward. Giving people something they needed and making them happy made him feel good about himself.

As word spread about what Trevor and his family were doing, others wanted to get in on the fun. "Hey, Trevor, can we come over this afternoon and help make sandwiches?" "Need anyone to help you serve food to the homeless? Papa said I could help." "My mom and I made a big pot of beans for you to feed to the homeless. We'll bring it over. What's your address?"

Soon, not only the kids from Trevor's school, but church groups and service organizations began volunteering to help Trevor's family make their nightly rounds. Others chipped in to keep their freezer filled with casseroles and homemade dinners. A couple vans were even donated to them, making it possible to meet the needs of more people.

Dad finally quit his job in the electronic field to help organize a non-profit organization called "Trevor's Campaign" to help the homeless. The city even donated a house for them to fix up and use as a place where the homeless could live for a while until they were able to get a job and find a place of their own. They called the house "Trevor's Place." The idea caught on, and soon there were nineteen homes around the country called "Trevor's Place."

Jesus told an interesting story to His disciples and friends that shows how important it is to help people like Trevor did. The story goes something like this: When the King of the universe comes back to earth in all His glory, everyone will be standing in front of Him and He will divide them into two groups. He'll call the group on His right the sheep and the one on His left the goats. To the sheep, He will say, "Come, you blessed of My Father, inherit the kingdom prepared for you." And to the goats, He'll say, "Depart from Me."

All the people will wonder *Why?* and the King will say to the sheep, "You fed Me when I was hungry, gave Me something to drink when I was thirsty, and gave Me a place to sleep when I was homeless."

The sheep people will ask Him, "When did we do that?"

The King will reply, "When you did it to others, you did it to Me. And because you were kind to others, you can come and live with Me forever." But to the goats, the King will say, "You didn't give Me food, water, or a bed, so I don't know you." And He will send them away.

Matthew, one of Jesus' disciples, was so impressed with this story that he wrote it down. You can read it in Matthew 25:31–46. Helping others is obviously very important to Jesus.

If you were to ask Trevor, "How old do you have to be to help others?" he would tell you that you're never too young—and you're never too old. In fact, Trevor is still helping others today. ■

> *Those who oppress the poor insult their Maker,*
> *but helping the poor honors him.*
> —Proverbs 14:31, NLT

The Flying Cat

Jillian was so excited about going to school that she put her shoes on the wrong feet and tied them before realizing her mistake. "Oh no!" she muttered, sitting back down on the entryway floor to fix them. For weeks she had been slaving at school in anticipation of this one glorious day—the fifth-grade winter party!

Not only did this day promise lots of cookies, cupcakes, games, and gifts, but it also launched winter break—two entire weeks off! After fixing her shoes, she stood up, grabbed her backpack, and announced to her parents that she was ready. She called twice to make sure they heard.

"We're coming, we're coming!" said her dad with a grin as he straightened his tie. "Your mom is almost ready." He put a hand on Jillian's shoulder and sighed. "I wish I got a winter party and two weeks off."

"I would love that! Just think of all the places we could go," Jillian said with a giggle.

"I doubt if you'll be going too many places over break since Dad and I have to work, but you better not be a couch potato either," said Mom, making her way out of the bedroom and slipping her shoes on in the entryway. "After vacation you'll have to go back to school, and I don't want you to forget everything you've learned."

"Mom, where's your faith in me?" laughed Jillian. "I have a super good memory, you know!"

"Glad you're so humble about it," joked her dad—then he looked at his watch. "Whoa! We are cutting it close! We don't want to be late for work." Jillian didn't need any more encouragement as she promptly grabbed the doorknob and flung the door open. But as she stepped triumphantly outside—so did someone else!

Pickles had come to live with Jillian's family six months ago on her birthday. She had always wanted a cat, and Pickles proved to be everything she had hoped for. Playful, loving, and curious, Pickles had provided hours of entertainment for Jillian and her parents. Generally speaking, Pickles behaved himself, however, he was notorious for two things: One, his unusual love for pickles, which is how he got his name, and two, his mischievous escape attempts. And this morning, in her excitement, Jillian did not see her kitty hiding behind Dad's winter boots. Pickles bolted as soon as she opened the door.

Everyone froze as they watched their orange striped cat sniff the fresh air and plot his next move. Jillian moved in slowly to grab him, but he skirted away, not interested in the constraints of the family's third-floor apartment. Jillian's apartment complex did not have indoor hallways like some did. Instead, it had stairways on the outside and a deck leading to the various apartments. What made the situation especially dangerous was the fact that the steps went down two floors, out into the parking lot— and then right into the street! The family was in a hurry, but any sudden moves might scare Pickles down the steps and into danger.

"Just play it cool, Jillian," suggested Dad. "Pretend like nothing is wrong, call him over, then pick him up, and put him inside." Jillian nodded.

"Here kitty, kitty, kitty," she cooed, taking a few steps toward the excited animal. But Pickles would have none of it. As soon as Jillian made a move, he raced down the outdoor hallway and around the corner. Jillian took off after him and found him backed against another apartment door.

Whew! thought Jillian. *He has nowhere to go. That was a close one!* Little did Jillian realize that her desperate pet did have one other option. As Jillian casually reached out to pick up Pickles, he darted to the left, through the railing, and jumped off the third-floor deck. Jillian gasped as she watched her precious pet fall through the air with all his little limbs spread out like a flying squirrel.

He's dead! He's dead! He's dead! she thought. Horrified, she watched him fall the thirty or forty feet to the ground, unable to tear her eyes away. But when he landed on the icy grass, he promptly got up, and darted away. HE MADE IT! Jillian couldn't believe her eyes. She raced back and told her parents what had happened. They were surprised. Then all three ran down the steps as fast as they could, calling for Pickles.

No luck.

Now a terrible sick feeling hit Jillian's stomach. He was nowhere to be found—not even a "meow." To make matters worse, even though he survived the fall, now he was on the ground with all the cars and not too far away from the busy road. And it was time to go.

Jillian's family only owned one car and both her parents needed to go to work—they were already late. Mom came over and hugged Jillian, who was fighting tears. "Sweetheart, I'm sure he's OK. But we need to go to work, and you have a party to get to." Dad gave Jillian a sympathetic expression and then walked over to where their car was parked and started it up. Jillian just shook her head.

"I'm going to stay home, Mom."

"What? Honey, today is the party! You have been really excited about it!"

Jillian wiped a tear away. "I know, Mom, but it's too dangerous if I just leave Pickles out here. I need to keep looking." Then she sighed and kicked a clump of snow. "Pickles! Why of all days did you choose today to run away?"

"Dad and I both have important appointments at work or we'd stay home with you," Mom said as she reached for her cell phone. "I'll call Mrs. Peterson and see if she can watch you until we get back." A few minutes later, it was all arranged. They were lucky to have a next-door neighbor who was almost always home—and loved having Jillian over.

Before Dad and Mom left, they put their arms around Jillian and prayed that God would keep Pickles safe and that Jillian would be able to find him. Then they waved to Mrs. Peterson who had come out on her deck to watch Jillian as she searched the parking lot for Pickles.

Jillian wandered around the large parking lot for nearly an hour looking for Pickles under parked cars and in the bushes. She called for him, but to no avail. Finally, she was so cold that she retreated inside where Mrs. Peterson gave her a big mug of hot chocolate.

"Why, oh why, today?" she muttered. "I bet everyone is having a great time at the party while I have to stay home looking for my silly cat who decided to escape!" She took a sip of her hot chocolate, then watched a few of the marshmallows dissolve. "I just hope Pickles isn't a pancake on the road." At this remark she started to cry. She loved her cat, but she was also angry, frustrated, and scared.

Mrs. Peterson came over and hugged her. "You'll find him. I've been praying too."

After calming down, Jillian put on her winter gear for another round of searching. She stepped outside the apartment and retraced her cat's escape route until she stood by the railing where he jumped off. She scanned the parking lot again. But where should she look? She had been everywhere.

Then, she heard a faint noise. It sounded like the whimpering "mew-mew" of a kitten. Jillian's heart leaped in her chest, and she nearly tripped and tumbled on her way down the steps to where she thought the source of the sound might be. Once on the ground she gently called, "Kitty, kitty, kitty," and waited, motionless.

Sure enough, the sound of a frightened cat came directly to her from a group of thorny bushes. Immediately, Jillian ran to the bushes, dropped down on all fours, and peered underneath. For a moment, she held back her excitement, half expecting to see the wrong cat. But as she gently moved some branches aside, there was Pickles. He was cold, huddled up, and meowing incessantly.

Since he wouldn't come out on his own, Jillian had to reach in and grab him. Even though she received several thorn pricks and scratches on her hands, she managed to pull out her beloved cat. Clutching him closely to her, she ran back to Mrs. Peterson's warm apartment, rejoicing. By the time she had warmed him up, fed him, and bandaged her hands, Mom and Dad came home for lunch.

"You found him!" exclaimed Dad as he picked up Pickles and petted him gently. Over lunch, Jillian recounted the morning's search. Then she spent a few moments playing with Pickles and his toys.

As Mom and Dad got ready to head back to work, Dad looked at his watch and said, "Run and get your coat, Jillian. If we hurry, you can make it back to school before the party ends!"

With Pickles sound asleep in his basket, Dad, Mom, and Jillian slipped quietly out the door and carefully locked it, leaving Pickles safe and sound in the apartment where he belonged.

"You know what," Jillian commented to her parents, "looking for Pickles reminds me of the story of the Good Shepherd looking for the lost sheep. I'm glad that Jesus is like that. It makes me feel safe knowing if I get lost, no matter how cold or stormy it is, or if Jesus has a party to go to, He will never stop looking for me until He finds me."

"That's a great lesson for all of us," Dad commented.

"I guess we have to thank Pickles for that one," smiled Mom.

As Dad pulled up to the curb next to Jillian's school, they stopped for a moment and bowed their heads as Dad prayed, "Thank You, Jesus, for helping Jillian find Pickles—and for being our Good Shepherd." ■

Then Jesus said to them . . . "I am the good shepherd. The good shepherd gives His life for the sheep."
—John 10:7, 11, NKJV

Brad's BMX Blunder

Brad leaned back in the recliner and flipped through the sports channels one more time.

"Brad, it's nearly eleven o'clock. You'd better start getting ready," called his mom from the study.

"Yep," said Brad, without moving from his comfortable chair.

Ten minutes later, his mother appeared in the doorway. "I'm serious, Brad. If you don't get organized soon we're going to be late for the race. Remember our deal about time management?"

"All right, all right," said Brad. "Just relax. We've got plenty of time. It'll only take me a minute to get my stuff."

Brad's mountain bike gear was stuffed in the closet in his room, along with all his other sporting equipment. Using his shoulder to push back the avalanche that threatened to spill out of the closet, he found his helmet and his shoes, but couldn't find his gloves. He stretched farther into the depths of

Photo taken by: Cori Hollingshead

the closet with no success. Brad gulped. The deal was that he could participate in mountain bike racing as long as he was ready on time. Managing time wisely was not his strong point. "Mom, do you know where my gloves are?" He cringed before she even replied.

"Bradley Michael Harrison, we are not having this conversation. You know the deal."

Brad fell backward onto his bed and groaned. He glanced at the clock on his bedside table: 11:37. How had that happened? Time just seemed to fly by and no matter how much he tried, he couldn't ever really get a handle on it.

Brad threw his gear into a bag. *Oh, great! Now I'll have to ride without gloves*. He high-tailed it to the garage and loaded his bike onto the bike rack. "Quick, Mom! We've got to get going or we'll be late."

Mom backed the car out of the driveway. She didn't say a word and Brad bit his tongue. He knew that was part of the deal too; Mom wouldn't drive any faster than the speed limit. It should only take thirty minutes to get to the track. Plenty of time.

It was the Under 14 Regional Championship and Brad had been training for six weeks. It was a new track and he needed to get there in time to register and have a practice run before the race. Picking the best lanes would give him a real shot at winning. He was the fastest in the competition, but with mountain biking, strategy was just as important as speed.

The traffic was horrendous, bumper to bumper all the way. "Where are all these people going?" questioned Brad impatiently.

"The new shopping center has opened down on East Street. They're having a family fun day today and there are big discounts at all the stores."

Brad frowned and crossed his arms across his chest. "I wish they'd get out of our way."

When they arrived at the track, there was a line to get onto the property, a line for parking, and a line for registration.

"Name?" said the official in the registration tent.

"Brad Harrison."

The man looked at his watch. "You made it with a minute to spare, son. Literally." He signed Brad's form and handed it back to him. "You won't have time to ride around the track before the race. Reckon you should have gotten here earlier."

"Plenty of time," said Brad with a laugh, but he felt his cheeks redden and turned quickly away.

At the starting line, Brad felt strange without his gloves, like he wasn't ready to race. He pushed the thought out of his mind and tried to concentrate. Without knowing the track, he would need a really good start if he was going to have a shot at winning. He decided he would follow whomever was in the lead and take it from there. If he timed it right, he would be able to pass the leader on the downhill run to the finish line.

His plan worked. He tucked in behind a guy in a green shirt riding a sweet, silver bike. Brad could tell the kid knew what he was doing and, more importantly, where he was going. The climb up the first hill was a breeze, but the second made Brad's calves sting. Although *Green Shirt Guy* was still in the lead, Brad could have passed him in a heartbeat—if only he knew where the track went next. Brad gritted his teeth and took out his frustration on the pedals.

The track took a turn to the left down through a rocky valley with a couple of nasty boggy sections. Brad followed *Green Shirt Guy's* lines through the mess and came out the other side unscathed.

MBBS3—7

As he crested the last hill, his knobby tire an inch away from *Green Shirt Guy's* back wheel, he saw the parking lot, the registration tent, and the finish line.

Green Shirt Guy chose the left hand run which had a couple of big boulders and some loose gravel. It looked like the better of the two options, but with no passing opportunities, Brad knew he couldn't win.

Brad steered his bike to the right where low, scrubby bushes grew. He pedaled flat out, his body tense and ready to react. In his peripheral vision, he could see *Green Shirt Guy* barrelling down the track. With a hundred feet to go, Brad dug deep and pushed the pedals harder, pulling ahead by the slimmest of margins. He could see the finish line, he could

see his mom cheering him on . . . but he couldn't see the large pothole dead ahead!

The sensation of flying through the air was a stark contrast to the heavy landing that awaited him when he hit the ground with a *thud!* His breath was knocked out of him. Brad groaned as the entire field of racers rode past him and crossed the finish line.

Dejected, embarrassed, and very disappointed, Brad wheeled his bent-up bike towards the car. He still had blood dripping from his knuckles. *If only I'd had time to find my gloves. If only I'd had time to ride the track first. If only! If only!*

The car ride home was quiet, but as they pulled into the driveway, Brad said, "Mom, I really messed up today."

"I'm just glad you weren't seriously hurt," said Mom, turning off the ignition. "That was a nasty crash. Honey, I know you think I'm hard on you about being punctual, but it really *is* something important. And it's not just because being late is an inconvenience to other people or adds stress to situations or, like today, leads to mistakes. It's because God wants us to use our time wisely. In Ephesians 5:15, the Bible tells us to be careful how we live; to be wise. Time management is part of that wisdom."

Brad lay in bed that night, his shoulders and knuckles throbbing from the fall. Mom was right. He had been anything but wise today, and he needed God's help. He prayed a silent prayer asking for wisdom and, in particular, help with managing his time. Then, Brad rolled over and set his alarm clock for half an hour earlier. He didn't want to be late for school tomorrow. ■

> *Be very careful, then, how you live—*
> *not as unwise, but as wise.*
> —Ephesians 5:15, NIV

Creampuff's Great Escape

Amber had lots of outside pets. There was her dog, Liza, and her three bouncing, begging Doberman puppies. And we can't forget the wild cat who lived in the barn with her three kittens who quickly hid behind the bales of hay every time she heard Amber calling her. Then there was Solomon, the big white cat, who ruled the house and the yard—including those boisterous puppies. But having dogs and cats that lived outside was not the same as having an indoor pet. So Amber talked her parents into getting Oscar, the fish who lived in a large aquarium in Amber's bedroom.

Oscar was amazing. He grew so fast and got so big that soon the aquarium was too small, and Oscar was eating Amber out of house and home. You see, Oscar ate live goldfish. At first, it wasn't so bad. Amber would save her allowance and buy a couple feeder fish each week for Oscar. But soon, Oscar was eating two fish a day! Oscar had to go. So Amber talked to her science teacher, Mr. Miller, and Oscar went to live in the classroom's big aquarium. Now Amber was lonesome once again for her very own bedroom pet.

That's how Creampuff became a member of the family's menagerie— which is a big word for a whole lot of animals.

Creampuff was a tiny cream-colored hamster. She was soft and cuddly and so tame that she would

just snuggle up in your hands and fall asleep. The first thing Amber would do after school each day was run into her room, open the cage door, and play with Creampuff. Sometimes, she even tried to do her homework with Creampuff running around her desk or trying to hide under her papers.

There was only one problem. Solomon was a great hunter. And he wasn't always an outside cat. He caught mice, rats, gophers, lizards, and sometimes even baby bunnies that lived in the orange groves around Amber's house.

You see, Solomon didn't know the difference between a little animal who was a pet and a wild animal who wasn't. To Solomon, *hamster dinner* was just as good as any other little animal that moved fast—but not fast enough to escape his claws and sharp teeth. So the rule was, if Solomon came indoors, Creampuff had to be put into her cage so she would be safe. And Amber always made sure the cage door was locked tight.

One day, after coming home from school, she did what she always did. She ran to Creampuff's cage to take her out and play with her. But where was Creampuff? The cage door was open and the cage was empty. Amber looked around her room. No Creampuff. She looked under her bed, behind her dresser, and under the pile of dirty clothes in her closet. No Creampuff.

Maybe her sisters were playing with Creampuff. She ran to find them.

Brooke was practicing the piano and hadn't seen Creampuff. Cori was out in the barn with her horse. She didn't know where Creampuff was either. Creampuff had escaped and no one, not even Mom or Dad, knew if Solomon had been in the house that day. And no one knew how the cage door got opened. It was a mystery.

Immediately, the whole family began to pray for Creampuff. "Dear Jesus, please help us find Creampuff before Solomon does!" And they made a new rule: *Don't let Solomon in the house until Creampuff is safe in her cage.* But what if it was too late?

The second rule was: *the door to Amber's room must be shut at all times.* They just hoped that Creampuff was still someplace napping in a cozy corner in Amber's room and was not running around the house where Solomon could eat her for lunch.

Amber could hardly sleep that night worrying about Creampuff. She was the best bedroom pet that Amber had ever had. She would never have another hamster as cute and tame and cuddly as Creampuff. "Dear Jesus," she prayed, "please help me find Creampuff."

The next morning, Creampuff was still missing. Amber searched everyplace she could think of before she had to leave for school. No Creampuff.

The minute Amber returned from school, she searched again, but to no avail. The family continued to pray that wherever Creampuff was, that she would be safe. They just knew a little hamster couldn't hide forever.

Amber was well aware that Creampuff loved to run around at night. So when she crawled into bed and turned out the lights, she tried to stay awake and listen for the sound of little hamster feet running around. But everything was quiet. And soon Amber fell asleep too.

At breakfast, the family decided to search the whole house for Creampuff. Brooke and Cori looked in their bedroom, Mom looked in the living room, Dad checked the study, and they all searched every possible hiding place in the family room and kitchen. No Creampuff. Where was she? Could she be in Solomon's stomach? *Yuck!* Amber couldn't bear that thought!

That afternoon, as Amber sat down to do her homework, she felt a little hungry, so she grabbed a crisp, red apple from the refrigerator and ate it while she figured out her math problems. When she was finished, she tossed the apple core into the wastebasket under her desk.

That evening, as Amber knelt beside her bed and said her good night prayers, she asked Jesus once again to help her find Creampuff. She knew that every day her hamster was missing there

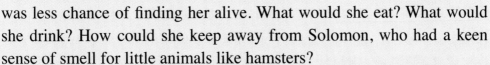

was less chance of finding her alive. What would she eat? What would she drink? How could she keep away from Solomon, who had a keen sense of smell for little animals like hamsters?

In the middle of the night, Amber was awakened by some scratching that sounded like it was coming from her wastebasket. At first, she was scared. Then she remembered Creampuff was missing. *Could it be?*

She flipped on the light and ran to the wastebasket and, sure enough, there was Creampuff, chomping away on the apple core.

"Mom! Dad!" Amber yelled so loud she woke up the whole family. "I found Creampuff! I found Creampuff!"

Creampuff's Great Escape

Everyone came running and was overjoyed to see Amber holding the now skinny, little hampster. After much petting and holding and nuzzling Creampuff's soft fur, Amber put Creampuff back in her cage, with water, extra food, and what was left of the apple core. Then she locked the cage door tightly—and checked it carefully to make sure there was no way a little hamster could open it.

That night, after thanking Jesus for answering their prayer, everyone slept safe and sound—including Creampuff. ■

For the eyes of the LORD are on the righteous,
And His ears are open to their prayers.
—1 Peter 3:12, NKJV

Teddy to the Rescue

W hen Grandpa Bob sat down in his big, brown leather recliner, Billy climbed into his grandfather's lap. "Grandpa, tell us a story," he begged.

Billy's older brother, Robert, plopped himself on the floor beside Grandpa's chair. "Yeah, Grandpa. Tell us a story—the one about Teddy!"

"Again?" Grandpa teased. "You don't want to hear that old story again, do you?"

"Yes, we do, Grandpa. That's my favorite." Billy snuggled down, resting his head on his grandfather's chest.

"Mine too," Robert echoed.

Grandpa chuckled and tousled Robert's hair. "Oh, all right. I guess Teddy's story is one of my favorites as well."

Grandpa cleared his throat and began, "When I was a small boy about your age, Billy, I lived in a house made of sod. Do you know what sod is?"

"Yep! It's mud!" Robert had all the answers. "We made one at school."

"Well, it wasn't exactly mud. It was more like the grass on your dad's lawn, with the roots and the dirt still attached." Though the boys had heard the story many times, Grandpa's explanation was an important part of the story for them.

Grandpa Bob continued, "The pioneers would dig up large, square chunks of the prairie sod or grass and stack it square upon square until it made a wall that was high enough to allow the farmer to stand up straight inside the house. Then the farmer would place a layer of boards across the top of two sod walls and stack more sod on top of the boards. The sod would keep the area inside the house warm in the winter and cool in the summer."

"And it had a dirt floor," Robert added.

"Hey, who's telling this story?" Grandpa teased.

"Sorry," Robert giggled.

Billy looked up at his grandfather and added, "Mom hates it when we track dirt in on her clean floor. Imagine how she'd feel if her floor was made of mud instead of tile."

Robert rolled his eyes and heaved a giant sigh. "Forget the dirt. Let Grandpa tell his story."

"Like all of our neighbors, my father built our house out of sod because there were so few trees on the Kansas prairie. Even obtaining enough wooden beams for the roof was very difficult," Grandpa admitted. "At that time there were no radios, no TVs, no video games, no cars, no cellphones—or telephones either, for that matter."

"What did you do with no TV to watch?" Billy asked.

"We read all kinds of books."

Robert nodded thoughtfully. "*Hmm,* that would be fun. I like to read."

"I do too, Grandpa," Billy added. "I read the most books out of all the kids in my class this year. I even got a special award."

"I know." Grandpa planted a kiss on the boy's cheek. "Your mom told me all about it. I'm very proud of you."

Robert gave a big sigh. "Can we get back to the story now?"

Grandpa chuckled. "Well, our little sod house didn't have running water or an indoor bathroom."

Robert interrupted, "You had to carry water in buckets from the well and you had to go outside and use the outhouse, even in the wintertime."

"Enough!" Billy wrinkled his nose. "I don't like outhouses. Remember the stinky one we used at the campground where we stayed last summer?"

Robert snapped his fingers. "Billy, let Grandpa tell his story!"

"My parents were called 'homesteaders.' " Grandpa adjusted his glasses on his nose.

"Homesteaders? What's that?" Billy asked.

"Homesteaders were pioneers who left their family and friends back east in cities like New York, Boston, and Baltimore and moved out west. Our family came from Albany, the capital of New York State."

"Why did they want to move?" Robert couldn't imagine leaving his parents, his grandpa, and all of his friends to live in a dirt house.

"The United States government offered free land to anyone brave enough to move out west and settle the land," Grandpa explained. "The pioneers were very resourceful. Besides using the prairie sod to build their houses, the land produced excellent green grass for the cattle during early spring and summer.

"The grass grew so tall and thick that sometimes Teddy my collie dog and I would play hide-and-seek in it or we'd lie down in the grass and stare up at the clouds and imagine they were dragons or dinosaurs."

"*Ohhh,*" Robert exclaimed, "that sounds like fun."

"It was! One summer I made an entire pretend city in the grass with pathways connecting each house."

"Tell about your mean neighbor, Grandpa," Billy urged.

"I'm getting to it, son. I'm getting to it." Grandpa continued. "Now, where was I? Oh, yes, I remember. Since only a few pioneer families had traveled west to settle, our closest neighbors lived ten miles away. We didn't see each other very much, unless someone needed help with a job that was too big for one family to handle, like building a house or a barn. Then we'd have what we called a 'barn-raising party.'

"Everyone in the county got along with one another pretty well, except for our closest neighbor, Mr. James, who loved cows and horses, but hated dogs."

A frown crossed Grandpa's face. "Whenever Mr. James would hitch up his horses to his wagon to come to our house for a visit, he would bring his long horsewhip. Of course, when Teddy heard the wagon coming, he would announce the visitor by barking. That annoyed Mr. James. So when he would pull his wagon into our front yard, he would snap the whip at Teddy. Sometimes it would actually hit him and Teddy would yelp in pain. Teddy wasn't used to people being mean to him. It didn't take him long to learn to bark from a distance whenever he saw Mr. James' buggy coming toward our house.

"One time, after Mr. James had visited us, he forgot his hat. Papa hung it on a nail so we would remember to give it to him when he visited us

again. Whenever Teddy spotted the hat in the barn, he would take off running, as if to avoid getting hurt by its owner's whip."

A deep frown crossed Billy's face. "I don't think I'd like Mr. James."

Grandpa patted his grandson on the arm and continued with his story. "One day, late in the summer after the grass had turned brown, storm clouds loomed on the horizon. The fierce storm hit around sundown. Tiny droplets of rain quickly became a downpour. Papa and I dashed for shelter as lightning flashed across the sky. Thunder shook the ground. We ran inside the house and barred the door."

"Barring the door means you locked it, right?" Robert asked, certain he knew the answer before he asked it.

"That's right. We dropped a heavy piece of wood across the doorway into a metal slot."

"Go ahead, Grandpa," Billy encouraged. "Tell about Teddy."

"It was very dark inside our sod house. Since we didn't have electric lights, and candles were difficult to read by, after supper everyone retired early. Teddy slept at the foot of my bed. In the middle of the night, when everyone was sound asleep, Teddy jumped down from my bed and let out a yelp that was followed by excited barking. My father said, 'Bob, tell that dog to be quiet!'

"I climbed out of bed and commanded, 'Teddy, be quiet! Go lay down!' But he wouldn't stop barking. Instead, he barked louder and lunged at the front door. 'Teddy, what is wrong with you?' I muttered as I shuffled across the floor to let Teddy out.

"Teddy bounded outside the house the

instant I opened the door. When I stepped outside to yell at the dog again, I spotted a distant prairie-grass fire burning to the west of our land. Lightning had ignited the dry grass. I shouted at my parents, 'Prairie fire! Papa, prairie fire's a comin'!'

"Papa leaped out of bed, shouting orders as he pulled on his shirt and trousers. 'Quick! Help me hook up the horses to the plow. We've got to plow a furrow around our house and barn and then start a backfire!' "

"A backfire," Robert explained to his younger brother, "is a fire started to burn the brush before the big fire arrives, so the big fire doesn't have anything to burn. Right, Grandpa?"

"Close, son, close," Grandpa said as he went on with his story. "Papa and I were harnessing our two horses to the plow when Papa spotted the hat in the barn and remembered that Mr. James didn't have a dog to warn him of the approaching fire. 'Get the hat and shake it in front of Teddy. Tell him to take the hat to Mr. James.'

" 'But, Papa, Mr. James doesn't like Teddy,' I protested.

"Papa replied, 'Can't be helped; he's our neighbor.' Obeying Papa, I whistled for Teddy to come. I had to tell him firmly several times before Teddy grabbed the hat in his teeth and ran off across the prairie toward Mr. James' house.

"All night Papa and I worked to keep the fire away from our house and barn. In the morning, we could see where the prairie fire had gone around our place. The backfires had done the job. Sweaty, smoky, and exhausted, we stumbled toward the house. Papa turned to inspect the burned land and spotted Mr. James' horse and buggy coming across the smoldering prairie. As the wagon drew closer, I could see that the hat Mr. James left at our house was on his head, and on the seat beside Mr. James sat Teddy, wagging his tail.

"Mr. James told us that when the dog started barking outside his house, he was angry and grabbed his rifle, intending to shoot the dog. But when he opened the door, he saw his hat in the dog's mouth and then he noticed the approaching fire. That's when Mr. James realized the dog had been sent to save his life. From that day on, whenever Mr. James came to visit, he brought Teddy treats—instead of whipping him. I think he was the only dog in the world Mr. James ever really liked."

Tears welled up in Grandpa Bob's eyes as he concluded his story. "Teddy was the best dog a fella could ever have. I will love that dog forever." ∎

Do not repay evil with evil or insult with insult, but with blessing, because to this you were called so that you may inherit a blessing.
— 1 Peter 3:9, NIV

Japanese Glass Float

"**O**h, look at this one, Mom. It's blue!" Kaitlyn called from across the cluttered shell shop. She lifted the large Japanese glass float into the air for her mother to see.

"That's a pretty one. But don't drop it!" Mom cringed, fearful that the giant, glass fishing float would slip from her daughter's fingers and crash to the floor of the shop. "It costs more than we can afford."

The shopkeeper inched closer, gently taking the glass globe from Kaitlyn's hands. "This is a particularly lovely one with the blue and green swirls in the glass. A local patron found it bobbing in the surf a few years ago."

"Really?" questioned Mom as she examined the glistening object. "It's beautiful! What I'd give to find even a small glass float on the beach!"

"When I was a kid," the shopkeeper explained, "my brother and I found them by the dozens. But today, they are quite rare, since most fishing boats use plastic floats for their nets. But if your eagle-eyed, occasionally ya can still spot one bobbing in the surf."

"Oh!" Kaitlyn's eyes danced with excitement. "I'd love to find one."

"Well," the shopkeeper warned, "ya gotta be careful along our Oregon coast. The Pacific Ocean is a jealous lady. Ya gotta treat her right. Once she gets hold of ya, she likes to keep ya." Suddenly, he grabbed Kaitlyn's shoulder with his gnarled fingers. Frightened, Kaitlyn pulled away in surprise.

The shopkeeper chuckled aloud. "Don't worry. If ya obey a few rules of the sea, you'll be safe."

"Rules?" Kaitlyn questioned. Rules sounded too much like school.

"Yes. Ya gotta watch Lady Pacific. She's a tricky one, especially when the tide is coming in. Ya may think that the waves can't reach ya, but as sure as ya turn your back, she'll sneak up behind ya and grab ya just like I did. Remember, rule number one is to never turn your back on the ocean."

"That's what my parents always say." Kaitlyn glanced toward her mother and laughed nervously.

"Listen to them. They're right. And here's rule number two: When wading, watch out for drop-offs. Lose your footing and ya can find yourself caught in a riptide and dragged far from shore before ya know what happened."

Kaitlyn nodded and backed away from the old man. "I spent my entire life on a fishing boat or living by the sea. I have a healthy respect for the ocean tides."

Mom held the float up to the light to enjoy the swirls and reflections in the blue-green glass. "This is a beauty, but a bit too pricey for my pocketbook. Besides,

MBBS3—8

I'd love to find one in the surf rather than purchase one." She returned the float to the counter.

The shopkeeper nodded, "It's a real beauty all right!"

Mom and the shopkeeper chatted for a few more minutes while Kaitlyn admired a display of seashells and sand dollars arranged by size, shape, and color. The bell over the shop door jingled. Kaitlyn turned to see Dad and her older sister, Amy, enter the shop.

"Hey guys, ready to go back to our campsite?" Dad asked. "We're hungry!"

"Dad bought homemade fudge for dessert." Amy waved a small white bag in the air.

"What kind did you get?" Kaitlyn lost interest in the shells as Amy peered into the bag and announced, "Chocolate walnut and peanut butter fudge!"

"Yum! Let's go." Kaitlyn bounded from the store.

After the short ride back to camp and a picnic lunch on the beach, the  girls begged Dad to hike with them up the hill to the lighthouse that overlooked the sandy cove.

"Sure, why not?" Dad laughed. "Gotta work off that yummy piece of fudge I ate."

"Just one piece?" Kaitlyn teased. "More like three!"

"Uh-uh! Two maybe." Dad scowled and then laughed. "But who's counting?"

"Mom, are you coming with us?" Amy asked as Mom placed her hat on her head and grabbed her sunglasses.

"I've been looking forward to building a sand castle on the beach," she said. "Why don't you go ahead?"

"Come on, Kaitlyn. I'll race you to that big pine tree. Bet I can beat you!" Amy pointed to a tall, slender evergreen halfway up the hillside.

"Oh, no you can't," Kaitlyn shouted over her shoulder as she dashed toward the narrow pathway leading to the lighthouse.

By the time Dad caught up, the girls were huffing and puffing at the base of the evergreen tree. "I'll race you to the top," he teased. Both girls groaned. "Come on, you two. On your feet, you can't quit now."

Exhausted, Kaitlyn and Amy scrambled to their feet and stumbled after their father, who maintained a steady pace up the narrow pathway. As they broke out of the woods into the clearing surrounding the lighthouse, the girls forgot how tired they were. The white lighthouse with black trim stood tall and majestic against the blue sky.

"Let's climb it." Kaitlyn ran to the fence surrounding the buildings where she found an iron padlock on the gate. "Ooh!" she groaned. "It's closed. The sign says it won't open until tomorrow morning at nine."

Disappointed, Amy's smile melted. "Dad, can we come back tomorrow when it's open?"

"Sure, why not?" Dad spent several minutes walking around the chain link fence, taking pictures of the lighthouse and the ocean beyond.

Bored, Kaitlyn broke into a run. "Amy, race you down the hill!"

"No fair! You got a head start!" Amy charged after her sister.

Kaitlyn raced down the narrow path leading to the beach where Mom's sand castle was taking shape. As she came around the bend, a glint of light from something bobbing on the waves caught her eye. *A Japanese glass float!* she thought. From what she could tell, the float looked to be as big as the one she had admired in the shell shop that morning. Without stopping, she shouted, "Mom! A float!" and dashed across the sandy beach and into the water.

"Kaitlyn!" Mom leaped to her feet. "Stop!" But the roar of the surf drowned out the sound of Mom's voice.

Focused on the object bobbing in the water, Kaitlyn bounded into the incoming waves. *I can make it! I can make it!* Kaitlyn told herself as she flung her body at the elusive float. Just as Kaitlyn grasped the gray-green float, the sand beneath her feet shifted and she plunged under the surging water. Sputtering and coughing, she fought to resurface. A receding wave dragged her into deeper water. Kaitlyn emerged ten to fifteen feet farther from the shore. Terrified, she clung to the fishing float and kicked with all her might toward shore. But she was not strong enough to compete with the powerful ocean current. She had barely caught her breath when another wave struck her. Water swirled about her head. She was going down again. Once more, she fought her way to the surface.

"Oh, dear Jesus, help me!" Kaitlyn cried, certain she would drown. This time, when she emerged, Kaitlyn could see Amy screaming and waving from the shoreline. Suddenly, another gigantic wave lifted her into the air like a rag doll and then plunged her beneath the ice-cold ocean water a third time. Still clutching the float to her chest, Kaitlyn felt a giant hand grab her by the back of her T-shirt and yank her toward shore.

Kaitlyn was too weak to help her rescuer paddle through the swirling water. Exhausted from battling the powerful ocean, her rescuer tossed her into the shallow water. It wasn't until her feet hit the sand that she realized . . . Dad had saved her! He had risked his life for hers. Before Kaitlyn could regain her footing, Mom rushed into the water, lifted her up, and hugged her tight.

"Oh, honey, I'm so glad you're safe." Mom cried between kisses and hugs. "Why in the world did you do such a thing?"

"But Mom, I found a Japanese glass float!" Kaitlyn held the fishing float up for her parents to see. Taking a closer look, she exclaimed, "Oh, no!"

The object she had risked her life for wasn't a beautiful Japanese glass float at all. It was a plastic float that had broken free from a Danish fishing buoy—and down one side of the gray-green globe was a jagged crack.

"Mom, it's ugly!" Kaitlyn wailed.

Mom brushed a lock of wet hair from Kaitlyn's face. "Forget the float. All that matters is that you're safe."

Kaitlyn struggled to her feet. "I was sure it was a Japanese glass float. It looked so real."

"I know, honey." Dad started toward the dry sand.

Once she was on the beach, Kaitlyn examined the float a second time. "What should I do with this ugly, old thing? Throw it away?"

"No, I think we should keep it," Dad said. "It can remind us of an important lesson. Jesus said something about the danger of gaining the whole world and losing one's soul. Sometimes the thing we think we want the most turns out to be worthless. And sometimes we act without considering the danger of making a bad choice. Kaitlyn, even if you had found the most beautiful float in the entire world, it wouldn't have been worth it if we had lost you! Your life is more valuable than any Japanese glass float!" ∎

> *What good will it be for a man if he gains the whole world, yet forfeits his soul?*
> —Matthew 16:26, NIV

Levi's Hockey Challenge

T he temperature had dropped below freezing and the ground was covered with snow. Suddenly, hockey was the topic all the kids were talking about. After school, Lou called, "Hey, Levi, are you coming down to the ice rink for hockey practice today?"

"Maybe," said Levi. "I'll have to ask my parents."

"I'm sure they'll say it's OK. Everyone in Woodland Park plays hockey, especially since we got the new community outdoor rink. Hope to see you there." Lou waved as he climbed into his dad's four-wheel truck and Levi headed to where his ride was waiting.

Levi really wanted to be a part of the in-group at school, and it seemed that all the guys played hockey. In fact, most of them had started skating when they were barely old enough to walk. Levi had just moved to Colorado a few months before and as far as playing hockey? Well, he had only been on skates a few times in his life. But Levi

was generally good at sports, so he wasn't really worried. That is, until he went to the first practice.

Levi stood at the side of the rink, amazed. Everyone, even kids much younger than he, was gliding around on the ice, skating this way and that, twisting, jumping, turning, and skating backward as if there was nothing to it. *How hard can it be?* Levi thought. *If they can do it, I can too.* Levi finished lacing up his skates and tried standing on the ice. *Oops!* He almost lost his balance. He grabbed the fence around the rink to steady himself.

"Go ahead and warm up," bellowed the coach to the team. "Five sprints and stops across the rink."

Five sprints and stops? thought Levi. *I can't even stand on these things. What am I going to do?*

Levi pushed off and started gliding on the ice, ankles wobbling, then took a step or two, while the others, including Lou, sailed past. Somehow, Levi managed to make it across the rink. He could hardly concentrate on his own skating because he was watching everyone else. Some of the guys were so good. He marveled at how they could be skating frontward and then, without any effort, turn around and skate backward.

In his head, Levi could see himself gliding across the ice, turning, reversing, hitting the puck, and making a goal. But the contrast between his daydream and how he really skated was as different as night and day. Gathering courage, Levi took a few more steps forward and tried to turn around on his skates, only to fall flat on his back, banging his head against the ice. "OUCH!" he cried.

His high expectations were crushed. Tears of disappointment formed in his eyes. He headed to the sidelines where his parents were sitting. "I can't skate backward like the other kids," he announced as he dropped his stick and plunked himself down on the bench. "This is harder than I thought!"

"Levi, don't be so hard on yourself. You've never had a chance to ice skate. You've lived in Tennessee all your life where the lakes never freeze. I bet the other kids can't wakeboard like you can. And most of them would be scared to death to jump off the rocky cliff into the lake or jump off the top of the boat dock like you do," his dad reminded him.

"I know, but I just can't seem to get the hang of skating backward."

"Levi," his mom added, "I know you have high expectations, but trying so hard to reach an unrealistic goal can crush your spirit and make you feel like giving up. Just go out there and have fun. Play around. Learn the basics little by little. And chances are, when you least expect it, you'll do it!"

A few days later, Levi and his family went to visit his cousins for Christmas. Fifteen-year-old Tristan, who had played hockey all his life, went through the hockey gear he had outgrown and wrapped it up for Levi. When Levi opened the big box on Christmas morning, he was thrilled. He immediately tried everything on. "Wow, I look like a real hockey player now—with breezers, elbow guards and knee pads, a jersey, and helmet. It fits perfectly," Levi beamed.

"Hey, I have an idea!" Tristan suggested. "Let's get our parents to take us to the rink in Nederland and try out some of this equipment."

"But I can't skate very well. I can't even skate backward," Levi complained.

"Don't worry, I'll show you how."

A couple of hours later, with hockey stick and puck in hand, the boys headed out onto the Nederland ice rink. "Levi, move your hips a little more. Push your legs out. You'll be surprised what a difference it will make," coached Tristan.

Levi tried, but once again, *BANG,* down he went. He was tempted to think, *I'll never learn.* But then he remembered the words of his parents, *Don't give up. You'll get it. Sometimes when you feel the weakest, just try harder and it'll happen. It's not always the natural athlete that excels in the end; it's the one who keeps practicing.*

Tristan skated up to Levi, who was lying flat on the ice. "Hey Levi, everyone falls when they're learning. No sweat, dude. You just have to keep trying," he said, giving Levi a hand. "Let's see how fast we can skate around this rink. Come on. Try to get this puck away from me. Push those legs. Faster! Faster!"

Levi began to fly around the rink. He felt the cold chill of the air sting his nose and cheeks. "Faster, Levi. Now swing your hips around." Levi tried, and before he knew it, he was moving backward across the ice.

Glowing with excitement, Levi shouted to his parents, "I got it! I got it! I skated backward!"

His dad gave him a thumbs up. "Son, we're really proud of you," he said as Levi plopped down on the bench beside them.

Just then, a teenage boy was practicing some fancy footwork down at the end of the rink away from the hockey players. "Levi, look at that guy's footwork," Mom pointed out. They sat watching as the boy crossed one foot over the other, circled, and glided backward and then forward. After about ten minutes, the boy skated over to the warming area where Levi was sitting with his parents.

"Great skating," Mom complimented the boy.

"Yeah," Levi added, "I'm just learning. I'd love to know how to do some of that fancy footwork."

"Really?" the boy said, pleased that others had noticed. "I'm Clint. What's your name?"

"Levi."

"Well, Levi, why don't you come out on the ice and I'll show you a few things."

"Wow!" said Levi. "That would be great!"

A few minutes later, Clint was mentoring Levi. "Try bigger swoops. Scoop more. Twist your body, lift your foot higher. Good! You're doing great! That's it. Scoop a little more. Hey, man, you're getting it. Do it again. Keep practicing."

Tristan skated over. "Levi, you're really looking good. You're going to make a terrific hockey player."

Clint agreed, "You're a fast learner, Levi. Just keep practicing."

"Thanks, Clint. I couldn't have done it without you . . . and Tristan."

Levi took a couple more swings with his stick, passed the puck back and forth to Tristan as they skated at a fast clip forward, and then turned around and skated backward with ease as his feet made large scooping motions. Next, he practiced some of the fancy footwork that Clint had shown him and then skated back to the warming hut.

"Dad! Mom! Did you see me?" he yelled, his face glowing with success—and the bite of the cold.

"Sure did," they called back. "Wow, it's amazing the difference a little confidence and a lot of practice makes."

Levi could hardly wait to go back to his next hockey practice in Woodland Park. As he skated up to his coach, he called out, "I want to show you something. I can skate backward now!"

Coach Dan watched in amazement. "I can't believe you're the same kid that showed up for hockey last week!" he exclaimed. "You've been practicing."

Levi flashed him a big smile—a winning smile—as he skated off to join Lou and the rest of the guys. ◼

> *Blessed is the man who perseveres under trial,*
> *because when he has stood the test,*
> *he will receive the crown of life that God has*
> *promised to those who love him.*
> *—James 1:12, NIV*

Katie's Colt

More than anything in the world, Katie wanted a horse. She dreamed about horses, she read books about horses, she talked about horses, and she drew pictures of horses. But all the dreams, stories, talk, and pictures only made Katie want a real live horse all the more. She even named the horse of her dreams; it was going to be Nikki!

When Katie was ten years old, her parents bought some property up in the mountains with an old log cabin, a horse shed, a spring, and a pond on it. A fence surrounded the entire property, which they called The Sky Ranch. And an old, black horse named Trigger came along with it.

The ranch was a perfect place to keep horses. Trigger was great for petting, but not for much else. What Dad wanted was a horse to carry the gear that he took on packing trips, so he went to a horse auction and came home with Beauty. Beauty was a small quarter horse with a black mane and tail. But the first time Dad tried to get

Beauty to carry a heavy pack, she lay down in the middle of the trail and wouldn't budge. Beauty was a great horse for riding, but she didn't like packing! So Dad went back to the horse auction and bought Buck, a big buckskin horse to carry heavy loads. Then, because he knew how much his daughter wanted a horse, he gave Beauty to Katie.

Katie was thrilled. At last her dream had come true. Every weekend, when she and her family would head up to the ranch, Katie would spend her time riding Beauty.

Beauty was only fourteen hands high. She was so small that Katie could easily jump on Beauty's back and ride bareback.

One day, when Katie and Beauty were galloping through an open field, an afternoon thunderstorm blew in. Suddenly, KABOOM! Lightning struck a tree close to them, scaring Beauty. She spooked and took off running even faster. Holding on for dear life, Katie managed not to fall off and they rode back to the safety of the shed at break-neck speed.

Another time, Katie was racing Beauty along a jeep trail. They had taken this route hundreds of times, and Katie just presumed Beauty would go straight like she always did. But for some reason, Beauty must have thought Katie nudged her to the right, so at full gallop, Beauty took the trail to the right, while Katie—went left. Katie rolled over and over in the dirt. Luckily, there were enough pine needles covering the ground that she wasn't seriously hurt. After a few minutes, Beauty returned and nudged Katie gently making sure she was OK, and together they rode back to the corral—this time a lot slower!

One weekend, when the family arrived at the ranch, the horses weren't there to greet them. That was strange. Katie called, "Beauty, Buck, Trigger!" Nothing!

Immediately, Dad and Katie jumped into the Jeep and drove all over the one hundred eighty acres looking for the horses, but couldn't find them anywhere. Katie started to cry. Where was her beloved Beauty?

"The horses must have found a place where the fence was down and wandered away," Dad said with a sigh. So they went to all their neighbors, asking if they had seen the horses. They looked in the adjoining pastures. They went all the way down to Jamestown, stopping at all the mountain cabins on the way. But no one had seen Beauty, Buck, or Trigger wandering around the mountain roads.

The next weekend, Dad and Katie hooked the horse trailer behind the Jeep and broadened their search. Still, there was no sign of the missing horses. Dad posted notices and told the sheriff. Six weeks went by. Katie had almost given up ever finding the horses, when she and Dad were slowly driving along a mountain road near the old town of Ballerade. Katie was calling, "Beauty, Buck, Trigger," as they went along. Suddenly, she heard a horse nicker. Dad stopped the Jeep, and Katie called again. Then, out from behind a clump of trees came Trigger, with Buck following after. Beauty, however, was not with them. That was strange. The horses always stayed together. Where could Beauty be?

Katie and Dad took Buck and Trigger to the ranch and after making

sure the gate was secure went back to search for Beauty. At last, they came upon a small log cabin inside the fence where they had found Trigger and Buck. Dad and Katie jumped out of the Jeep and knocked on the weathered door. An old mountain man called out in a gruffy voice, "Whatcha want?"

The door creaked open as Dad started to explain. After the story about finding Trigger and Buck inside the old man's fence, the mountain man admitted, "Yeah, I found them horses wandering down the road and put 'em inside my fence so they wouldn't get hit."

"Was a small, brown mare with them?" Katie asked.

"I don't rightly recall," the old man said hesitantly.

"She had to be. Those horses always stay together. She's got to be here somewhere!"

"Haven't seen no mare," the man insisted.

Dad wouldn't take no for an answer. "We know she's here. Tell us where she is."

"Where's Beauty? She's my horse!" Katie pleaded.

"There were only two horses," the man insisted. But when Dad kept asking questions, the old man changed his story and said, "Oh, are you talking about that little mare that I put in with my stallion? She's back in the barn out yonder. She's going to have a foal early in the spring."

At first, Katie was excited about the news of the foal, but then she and her dad decided that the old man didn't always tell the truth and this was probably just another one of his stories. But regardless, Katie was happy. She had her horse back.

That winter, Dad trailered the horses down to a pasture closer to town and paid a farmer to feed them. Katie had not seen her horse for months so she soon forgot all about the story of Beauty having a foal.

One day, in early spring, when the cold wind was blowing and snowflakes were swirling, the farmer called. "I just went out to feed your horses—and that mare of yours has a newborn colt."

"So it really was true!" Katie exclaimed.

Katie bundled up in her winter jacket, hat, and mittens, and she and her dad took the long drive to where the horses were being boarded. Sure enough, out in the field was the most beautiful colt Katie had ever seen. She was overjoyed. Not only did she have Beauty, but now she had a long-legged, little brown colt with a white blaze down his face and three white socks. He was beautiful! And she didn't have to think twice. "I'm going to call him Nikki," she announced.

Katie tried to get close to Beauty and the colt, but the horses were skittish after not having been ridden for six months. So Katie and her dad just watched them for a while, took some pictures, and headed back to town.

The next day, Dad was extra busy and couldn't take Katie out to see her colt. Katie wished she was old enough to drive there by herself, but she would just have to wait for her dad. Then the next day, just as they were getting ready to go out and check on Nikki, they got another call from the farmer. "Hey," he said, "I don't know what happened, but your colt is dead."

"No! No!" cried Katie. "It can't be true!" But it was. When Katie and Dad arrived at the pasture, there was the beautiful, little colt lying cold and stiff on the frozen ground. Dad and the farmer began to talk about what could have happened. The only explanation they could come up with was that no one had ever seen the colt feed. "I have a feeling," the farmer said, "that this is the first foal that your mare has had—and she didn't know she needed to let the colt nurse. It happens sometimes."

Katie cried herself to sleep that night. She had swollen, red eyes when she went to school the next day and she couldn't concentrate on her classes. All she could think about was Nikki. Why didn't she and her dad wait long enough out there in the pasture to make sure the colt was nursing? It's always sad when a pet dies, but what made it even harder for Katie was that it could have been prevented, if she had only known!

The days went by and soon it was summer. Dad suggested, "Maybe we should breed Beauty. What do you think about her having another foal?"

"That would be awesome!" Katie beamed with excitement.

They found a good stallion, and, each month, Katie grew more excited as Beauty's belly got bigger and bigger with the foal growing inside of her. Dad found a winter pasture closer to their house so that they could check on Beauty every day. Then on a warm, sunny day, early that next summer, Beauty had a precious, little sorrel filly with a blaze down her nose. Once more, Katie named the foal Nikki.

Katie and her dad were there when Nikki stretched her front legs and stood up for the first time. Then, Nikki turned to her mom and started to nuzzle her, looking for some warm milk. But Beauty moved away. She was doing the same thing that she had done with her first foal. This time, Dad and a couple of his friends were ready. They put a rope around Beauty's neck and hind quarters and tied her to the side of the barn so she couldn't move away when the foal started searching for the warm milk. Once again, Nikki got close to her, and Beauty tried to move—but she couldn't. When Nikki's tummy was full, Dad and his friends untied Beauty and watched as she let her baby nurse again. At last, Beauty had learned how to be a good mother. And Katie had learned a valuable lesson about life and death.

Because we live in a sinful world, bad things sometimes happen. Pets sometimes die. But the Bible says in John 16:20, "Your sorrow will be turned into joy." And that's exactly what God did for Katie. ∎

> *You will be sorrowful,*
> *but your sorrow will be turned into joy.*
> —John 16:20, NKJV

MBBS3—9

Gavin's Gift

Tragedy struck the Gilbert home just before Thanksgiving and, suddenly, the family found themselves penniless. They were feeling the financial pressure that comes when there is more money going out . . . than there is coming in. And Christmas was right around the corner.

Gavin's little brother, Curtis, knew times were difficult, but he had his heart set on getting a bicycle for Christmas. For a year, he had been riding around the neighborhood on his old, rusty, banged-up scooter. In fact, he rode that scooter so much that his family had begun teasing him that his left leg was going to be permanently shorter than his right. Curtis tried to be content with his scooter, but with every push, he dreamed of the awesome BMX bicycle that he knew was for sale at the store. It was shiny and green and had trick bars on both the front and back wheels.

"Do you think I might be able to get it for Christmas?" Curtis would ask. Dad's standard answer had been, "Maybe. You'll just have to wait and see." But after the November disaster, Dad had begun to say, "Curtis, there isn't any money for a bicycle this year, so don't get your hopes up."

The first time Dad said this, Curtis was so disappointed. He went to the bedroom he shared with his younger brother and cried his eyes out. "It's not fair. It's just not fair," he kept saying. "I've waited so long. It's all I want for Christmas."

Gavin tried to make Curtis feel better. "Don't worry," he said. "Christmas is going to be wonderful. Just wait and see."

"How can you say that? Dad said there wouldn't be a bike, and I've waited so long—I don't think I can wait any longer."

"Well," said Gavin, "what if I take your old scooter and fix it up for you? Maybe I can get Dad to help me get the dents out and paint it up. What color would you like?"

"I want it to be blue," Curtis said as his eyes looked hopeful, "just like Uncle Scott's Harley-Davidson motorcycle, with a siren and some red lights or at least reflectors on the front so it would be like a policeman's motorcycle."

"I don't know if I can do all that since it's only three weeks till Christmas," Gavin said, "but I'll try."

"Thanks," Curtis said as he wiped a tear from his eye, "but I still really, really, really want a bike."

Gavin took Curtis' old scooter out to the workshop behind the garage and started sanding off some of the chipped paint. He planned to ask his dad to help him with the rest. But the more he sanded, the more he heard his brother's sad, little voice saying, *But I really, really, really want a bike.*

That night, as Gavin was finishing his homework, he happened to stop by the bedroom where Mom was putting Curtis and his baby brother to bed. He listened at the door and overhead Curtis praying. "And please, dear Jesus, You know I really, really, really want a bike for Christmas, but if I only get a fixed-up scooter, I guess it's OK. Amen."

Suddenly, Gavin got an idea. *I wonder how much a bike costs?* he asked himself. He decided that the next time someone in the family was going to town, he would ask to go along and check out the cost of a bike. There were only three weeks left before Christmas. Maybe, just maybe, he could scrape together the money.

For the past year, Gavin had been wanting an iPad. "It seems like all the cool kids at school have them. If I earn the money, can I get one?" he had asked his parents. "You can do everything on them—surf the Internet, watch videos, download games . . . it's amazing."

His parents had told him that he could get one if he would earn the money for it. He had been saving for it ever since, doing odd jobs around the neighborhood. He had even gotten a Sunday paper route and in the summer had handed out a flyer that said he was willing to take care of plants and pets for people going on vacation. He knew that soon he would have enough money to make his dream come true.

But the more he thought about it, the more impressed he became that although he wanted an iPad, he couldn't imagine it making him as happy as watching Curtis on Christmas morning. Gavin smiled to himself as he thought about how excited his little brother would be to discover a bike under the Christmas tree instead of a painted-up, old scooter.

When he got to his room, he took down the jar from the shelf where

he kept his savings. He locked his door, then sat down on his bed, dumped out the jar, and began counting. He had already given tithe on this money, so he could use every penny for the bike.

The next day, he hitched a ride with his uncle Scott on his Harley-Davidson and headed down to the bicycle shop. Uncle Scott helped him locate the exact bike that Curtis had been dreaming of. He checked the price tag. *Even with tax,* he thought, *I think I'll have just enough.*

When he told Uncle Scott that he was planning to surprise Curtis with a new bike, his uncle offered to help him put it on lay-away. They made arrangements to come down the day before Christmas and pick up the bike in his truck and hide it at his place until Christmas morning. Gavin was ecstatic.

One by one, the days seem to slowly pass by. Finally, ten more days until Christmas. Then five . . . four . . . three . . . two . . . and one. And every day Curtis would ask, "Hey, Gavin, how's the scooter coming?"

"Fine," Gavin would say. He wanted Curtis to believe he was working on it, so Curtis would think the scooter would be his Christmas gift.

Very late Christmas Eve, when Curtis was fast asleep, Uncle Scott helped Gavin roll the new bike into the living room and then place it strategically under the tree. Mom made a red bow and put it on the handlebars along with a big tag that said, To Curtis . . . From your big brother. Gavin could hardly get to sleep thinking about how surprised Curtis would be.

In the next bedroom, Curtis was sound asleep dreaming about the almost new scooter that he was sure would be under the tree, thanks to Gavin.

At the first light of dawn, Curtis got up and headed down the stairs toward the Christmas tree. He could hardly wait to see what Gavin had done to his scooter. At first glance, he didn't see it. *I wonder where it is?* he thought as he went around to the front of the tree. "What?" Curtis hollered so loud that Gavin heard him all the way in his room. He jumped out of bed and ran to the top of the stairs, just as Curtis began yelling, "Mom, Dad, Gavin, come quickly. It's a bike! It's a bike! It's a real bike!"

As the family gathered around, Curtis kept exclaiming, "It's the most beautiful bike in the world!" Then, even though it was a frosty cold day, Curtis hurriedly put on his big boots and his heavy jacket over his pajamas and started riding his bike around the yard and down the driveway. What a Christmas! The best ever!

"Well, Gavin," Mom and Dad said as they stood at the window watching Curtis making figure eights on his bike in the driveway, "any regrets?"

"Nope, not one bit," he said emphatically. "I can earn the money for an iPad again, and seeing the joy on Curtis' face when he first saw his new bike . . . makes it worth it all!" ∎

> *Give, and it will be given to you.*
> *For with the same measure that you use,*
> *it will be measured back to you.*
> —Luke 6:38, NKJV

Birthday-in-a-Box

"**T**his girl's name is Elena," Grandpa said as he was showing Jada and Darnell the photos he had taken on his latest trip. Grandpa drove a truck for a special project that helped poor people who didn't have enough to eat.

"When I get to the food depot, the first thing we do is unload all the supplies. It usually takes all day, so when we're finished, Elena's family always invites me to stay with them. They used to live in a big house with lovely things, but when they came to this country they had to leave almost everything behind. They could only bring one suitcase each."

Jada tried to imagine what she could fit into one suitcase. She would have to leave most of her toys behind. "That must have been awful!"

"Yes, it was terrible," replied Grandpa. "Elena's mom volunteers at the food depot so she can make sure her family has rice, beans, and milk every day."

"Is that all Elena has to eat?" Darnell wrinkled up his nose.

"Pretty much. They don't have enough money for all the yummy food you and Jada like."

Grandma put a big box down on the floor. "I've got a wonderful idea!" she said with a sparkle in her eye. "Elena has a birthday right after Grandpa's next trip. Wouldn't it be fun if Grandpa could take her a present from us?"

"What can we send?" wondered Darnell. "Maybe she'd like one of my soccer balls?"

"That would be nice for a start, Darnell," said Grandpa. "Let's put our thinking caps on and come up with something really, really special."

After a short pause, Grandma continued, "I've got an idea. What about a Birthday-in-a-Box?" Grandma loved planning surprises.

"What's a Birthday-in-a-Box?" asked Jada.

"It's everything you need for a fantastic birthday party. Can you imagine what Elena's birthdays have been like? Ever since she came to this country, there's never been enough money for a party, probably not even enough for a cake! She never has new clothes or new toys. Her family has to buy everything in second-hand stores."

By this time, Jada and Darnell were bubbling over with ideas. "A whole party in a box," said Jada, "with candy, and gum, and balloons . . ."

"And party bags with little treats," interrupted Darnell. "They're the best!"

Grandma smiled and started writing the suggestions down. "What else should we send?"

"Invitations!" yelled Jada. "Really pretty pink ones!"

"Good idea, Jada," said Grandma. "I wouldn't have thought of those!"

"I have lots that were leftover from my birthday party. They're in my closet at home. Remind me to get them when you take Darnell and me home."

"I wonder what Elena likes to eat at parties?" Grandma asked as she went to the pantry and started taking boxes and plastic containers of food off the shelves. She piled an armful on the table and started sorting through them.

"Pudding, for sure!" Darnell picked up a box of lemon pudding. "Yum! My favorite!"

Jada picked up a jar. "And peanut butter for peanut butter and jelly sandwiches would be good."

"And it also makes great cracker towers," added Darnell as he picked up a box of crackers.

Soon, they had a pile of pink-iced cakes, chips, crackers, granola bars, and cartons of juice ready to stuff in the box.

"We must buy Elena some birthday presents too," said Jada. "I want to buy her an art set because she likes to draw. Grandpa said so!"

"I like to draw too," Darnell added.

"But it's not your birthday, silly!" Jada teased.

"Hey, Grandma, why not buy Elena some dollhouse furniture and some tiny dolls?"

"I've been making a list of all the things you kids have suggested," said Grandma. "Let's head to the store and see what we can get to fill up the rest of the box."

When Grandma and Grandpa drove the children back to their home, Jada raced upstairs to find the leftover invitations. As she searched through her clothes hanging in the closet, she noticed a beautiful party dress. She had never worn it before. In fact, the price tag was still on it. She loved this dress and was saving it for a special occasion.

Oh, Elena would love this dress! She took it downstairs, and Mom helped her to wrap it in white tissue paper and put it in a pink box with a pretty ribbon while Darnell wrapped up the art set.

The next time they visited Grandma and Grandpa's house, they took their pretty wrapped presents and put them in the birthday box. Grandma wrote a letter explaining what the box was for and laid it on the very top. Then they taped up the box and wrote, "USE FOR ELENA'S BIRTHDAY" on every side.

Soon it was time for Grandpa to start the long journey in the truck. The whole family came to say Goodbye. He put Elena's box in a safe place behind the passenger seat.

The family made a circle around Grandpa and prayed he would be safe and that the truck wouldn't break down. Darnell prayed that the Birthday-in-a-Box would be Elena's best birthday ever! And then they waved until Grandpa's truck disappeared around the corner.

"You know," said Darnell, "I think I had as much fun making the Birthday-in-a-Box as I did having my real birthday!"

Jada smiled, "And so did I! Isn't that funny?"

When Grandpa got to the food depot, he waited until Elena's mom wasn't looking and put the box on her desk. When her mom opened it and read the note, tears of joy filled her eyes. *My daughter will have the best surprise birthday party ever.*

On the day of her birthday, Elena woke up and stretched. This was

supposed to be a special day, but she wasn't excited. Before they came to America, her birthdays were really special. There was always a beautiful, new dress, a party with all her friends, and a pile of lovely presents. But now her family was poor. All she got for her last birthday was a candy bar and some toys from a yard sale.

I wish I could have a party, Elena thought, *but I know it's impossible.* Sometimes she wished they had never come to America. Mom wasn't allowed to have a job that paid money and Dad had to work hard to pay for his studies as well as their rent and other expenses.

Suddenly, her bedroom door opened and in came Mom and Dad, smiling and singing! Mom had her arms full of pretty wrapped presents. "Happy Birthday, Elena!" Elena was so surprised! She unwrapped each present carefully, saving the pretty paper and ribbons. There was the most beautiful dress ever; a set of dollhouse furniture and some dolls; a gorgeous art set; a game she had always wanted; and several other wonderful things, including a soccer ball!

Then Dad said, "Elena, this afternoon I'd like to take you to the zoo. A friend in my class works there and he gave me some free tickets. How about it?"

Elena was overjoyed!

When they came back from the zoo, Dad gave Elena the key to the apartment. "Run up and open the door," he said. "I need to check the mailbox."

Elena opened the apartment door. Suddenly, all her friends jumped out from behind the furniture and yelled, "Surprise! Happy Birthday, Elena!"

She couldn't believe her eyes! There were pink balloons and party decorations everywhere. The table was full of wonderful treats. Mom's eyes were shining with delight. Elena ran to her room, put on her new dress, brushed her hair, and had the best birthday party ever! She was amazed when Mom brought out beautiful party-favor bags packed with lovely toys and candy to give to all her friends!

After the party, Elena helped Mom tidy up. They rolled up the party decorations to use again next year. Then Elena gave her mom a big hug. "Thank you so much for my party! It's been the most wonderful party ever! But how did you afford all this?"

"Well," said Mom, "someone sent you a Birthday-in-a-Box! I have no idea who it was. A box with your name on it just turned up in the food depot with all the decorations, your dress, invitations for your friends, party games, favor bags, and some extra money so we could buy you some presents, a cake, and some ice cream too!"

Elena went to sleep with a smile on her face. If there were people kind enough to send her a Birthday-in-a-Box, maybe life in America wouldn't be so bad after all! ■

> *Give to the poor,*
> *and you will have treasure in heaven.*
> —Mark 10:21, NKJV

Paint Thief

David wanted to do what was right—but it seemed like he was always getting into trouble. He grew up in a neighborhood where the kids ran the streets and did whatever they wanted to do without much— if any—adult supervision. His mom worked all day and sometimes all night; and when she wasn't working, she was often sick. David hadn't seen his dad in years. His older brother and sisters were supposed to keep an eye on him, but that proved to be an impossible task.

One day, as David was walking down the street, he heard a loud *crash,* then the shattering of glass. Then he heard it again. He ran around the corner and saw some of his friends throwing rocks at the small windowpanes in an abandoned building. As soon as they saw him, they yelled, "Hey, bet you can't hit a window!"

David hesitated just a moment. *What should I do,* he wondered. *I don't want these guys to think I'm a wimp.* Without another thought, he gathered a pile of rocks and started throwing them toward the window. *Crash, shatter, clunk!* His aim was right on target. The boys egged him on. "Hey! You're pretty good! Throw some more! Why don't you try and hit that one over there?"

David's conscience pricked him a little. He knew he shouldn't be destroying property. *I'm just a kid having fun and there's nothing else to do,* he told himself. But when someone yelled that the patrol car was coming, he took off running just like the rest of the boys.

Moments later, as he was walking along the street still a little out of breath, a policeman drove up to him and asked, "Hey, kid! Were you with the gang who was breaking windows?"

David shook his head *No* and tried to look surprised. "My mom's in the hospital and I was just walking home, minding my own business."

"Well, if I catch those kids, they'll be in big trouble! They're a menace to this community," the policeman threatened as he drove away.

This wasn't the first time David had lied his way out of trouble. Somehow, each lie seemed to get easier and easier.

A few weeks later, David's teacher announced that for the next art project each student would need to purchase three tubes of oil paint. David wanted to get an A on the project, but he didn't have the money to buy the paint he needed. He delivered papers for extra spending money, but he wouldn't get paid for a couple of weeks. He decided to go down to the art supply store and find out how much the paint cost.

When he entered the store, no other customers were in sight, and the clerk was busy framing a picture. David hurried to the aisle where the art supplies were kept and found the paint he needed. He picked up a tube and checked the price. *It's not as expensive as I thought. I'll have plenty of money to buy it when I get paid next week. But I can't wait till then! It will be too late!* Then he had a tempting thought. *Why wait? I need it now, and it's not really that much money. That old clerk probably won't even realize it's missing!*

He looked around to make sure no one was watching, then quickly stuck the three tubes in his pocket and walked out of the store. He finished his art project and was quite pleased with himself when he received an A for his painting. But the next week when he got paid for his paper route, he decided against paying for the paint. *If I go back and give the clerk the money, he might call the cops! It's not worth going to jail!*

No matter how hard David tried, he just couldn't seem to stay out of trouble. He didn't see the point of trying to be good if he didn't have a family that cared. One day, David's neighbor, Mr. Johnson, asked David if he would like to attend a Christian school. "I'll pay your tuition, but you need to promise to study hard and obey the rules."

"You bet I will!" he responded. He was excited to think someone cared enough to pay for him to go to a private school. David loved it there and he especially loved his Bible classes. He began to learn about God and how much Jesus loves him. He was fascinated with the stories of Noah, Moses, and Daniel, and he wished he could be more like them. But most important, he learned about what Jesus had done for him when He died on the cross. The more he studied, the more his love for Jesus grew, and so did his desire to keep all of God's commandments.

The first semester flew by and soon it was time for winter break. It was the day before Christmas and David's family had gone to the mall to do some last minute shopping. Since the house was quiet, David decided he would spend his time reading his Bible and praying. He tuned in to a Christian radio station that was playing Christmas carols. David began to listen to the words of the songs. Then he turned to the book of Luke and began reading the Christmas story. He thought about how Jesus had given up so much to come to this world as a tiny baby who was born in a lowly manger. When he read how Jesus gave His life on a cross so that his sins could be forgiven, his eyes filled with tears. That's the part that really touched David's heart. He felt terrible that he had done so many bad things. *Dear Jesus,* he prayed, *please forgive me.*

David suddenly remembered the three tubes of oil paint that he had stolen. He knew Jesus would want him to do the right thing and pay what he owed. No matter how much he tried to push it out of his mind, he just couldn't stop thinking about it.

What should I do? he thought. Instantly, he knew he *had* to make things right. He couldn't wait another minute. David quickly reached under the bed and retrieved the box where he had hidden the money his grandma had sent him for Christmas. *This should be enough,* he thought. Then he grabbed his winter jacket and quickly walked the few blocks to town. When he reached the art supply store, it was already dark. It hadn't dawned on him that it would probably be closed on Christmas Eve. *Now what should I do?* he wondered.

He didn't want to wait another day! He just had to make it right. He took the crumpled bills out of his pocket along with a scrap of paper and a pencil and began to write: "Dear Sirs, Last year I stole three tubes of oil paint from your store. Since then, I have given my life to Jesus and I want to be more like Him. That's why I need to pay you for the paint.

This should be enough to cover the cost. Please forgive me." Then David carefully wrapped the paper around the money and stuck the note in the crack of the door.

Just as David stepped back from the recessed door, he noticed a policeman watching him. *Oh, no! The cop probably thinks I am trying to break into the store.* David walked up to the policeman and said, "I wasn't doing anything bad, I promise. I just left a note for the owner and some money."

The officer walked up to the door and pulled out the paper to see if David was telling the truth. He read the note, took a deep breath, and said, "Son, you did the right thing and I'm really proud of you."

David's heart was singing all the way home. He bounded up the stairs and into the house, praising God. *Thank You, Jesus, for giving me the courage to make it right! And thank You for forgiving me.*

The next day, David noticed the headlines of the newspaper lying on the kitchen table, "Boy Returns Money," and below was a photograph of his note to the store owner. At first, David was embarrassed that others would know what he had done. But, as he read the article, he realized that maybe it would help someone give their heart to Jesus. David smiled to himself. This is going to be the best Christmas ever! ∎

> *Therefore, if anyone is in Christ,*
> *he is a new creation; old things have passed away;*
> *behold, all things have become new.*
> —2 Corinthians 5:17, NKJV

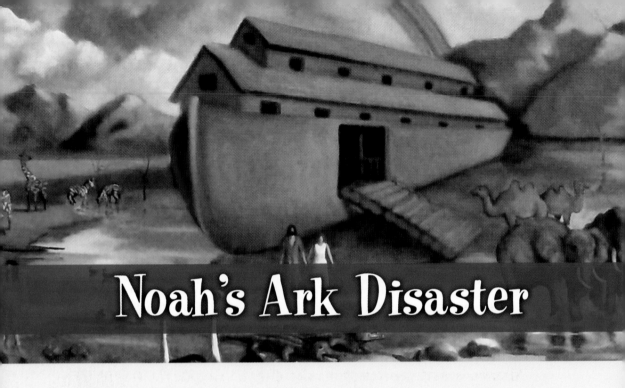

Noah's Ark Disaster

Breakfast was over, and Mom was issuing last minute orders as she began loading the dishwasher. "Kids, company will be here soon. Get your rooms clean. There will be a *white-glove inspection* in an hour. No dust anywhere. Do you understand?"

The kids hurried to finish making their beds, picking up dirty clothes, and dusting the furniture.

Uncle Jack, Aunt Doris, and Cousin Larry from California had never visited Colorado, so this was a very special occasion. Mom had declared that everything was to be PERFECT. The lawn had been mowed and edged, the dandelions pulled, and the windows washed. And just to make sure the living room would be spotless, Mom had even paid to have the carpet professionally cleaned. That had never, ever happened before!

"They're here! Mom, they're here!" shouted Ricky, who had been watching for their car to pull into the driveway.

Noah's Ark Disaster

"Quick! Quick!" shouted Mom to Julie. "Please put the dry dishes in the cupboard while I run out and greet everyone. And Ricky, call Dad at work and tell him to hurry home. Uncle Jack's here!"

In a flash, everything was put away. *Wow!* thought Julie as she rushed through the living room to greet the relatives coming up the porch steps, *I've never seen this place look so good!*

After hugs and kisses, everyone sat down in the spick-and-span living room to enjoy the fresh lemonade Mom had made. Dad soon arrived and made a suggestion, "What about going to see Flagstaff Summit before it gets dark? The view from the top is spectacular."

"Great idea," replied Uncle Jack. "We'd love to spend some time in the mountains."

"Who all wants to go?" Dad asked.

Everyone wanted to go. Everyone, that is, except Julie. She had been to the top of Flagstaff zillions of times—and besides, she got carsick going around all those curves. Plus, she had a project she wanted to work on without her little brother and sisters bothering her.

"I think I'll stay home and make that Noah's ark backdrop I've been asked to do for the church play Friday night," she said. "Besides, if I don't go, you can all crowd into one vehicle."

"OK," said Mom. "We'll be home in about three hours. If you need anything, call my cell phone."

Julie loved being home alone. The house was so quiet, and there was no one to tell her what to do. It made her feel all grown up. She got out the two white bed sheets that she had stitched together and spread them out on the floor. She had planned to use colored chalk to draw Noah's ark on the sheets, thinking she could work on the vinyl floor in the kitchen, but there wasn't enough room. She went outside on the patio. It was big enough, but the flagstones made such a rough surface that it would be difficult to make a nice looking picture. She came back inside. *What should I do?* The living room floor was the perfect size—too bad it had wall-to-wall carpet that had just been cleaned.

If only she had thought to ask Mom if she could make the backdrop on the living room floor. Her conscience told her that using chalk in the living room was not a good idea. *But,* she argued with herself, *what would it hurt?* She could put newspapers down around the edges to make sure no chalk got on the rug. And, if a little got on the carpet, she could vacuum it up, and Mom would never know.

And so, in the end, Julie spread out the sheets on the carpet and sketched out a Noah's ark that covered the entire backdrop. It was huge. She took out brown chalk and colored it in. Then she made blue, wavy water for the ark to float on. She completed the picture with a brightly colored rainbow in the sky.

At last, Julie stood up and surveyed her work. *What an incredible picture,* she thought. *It almost looks real. Having this backdrop will make the play so much more realistic.* She was quite proud of herself. She could just hear the *ooh*s and *aah*s coming from her friends when they would see her picture.

She made a few more finishing touches, then took out the spray fixative and began to spray it over the chalk drawing. The fixative would hold the chalk in place so it wouldn't smudge when the backdrop was taken to the church and hung on the wall.

Julie waited about twenty

minutes for her picture to dry. It was almost time for everyone to return. She carefully began to pick up her backdrop. What she saw on the floor, however, made her heart leap in agony. The chalk dust from her drawing had gone right through the sheets and onto the carpet! She couldn't believe it! There, on the professionally cleaned carpet, was Noah's ark, so clear that it looked like she had drawn it directly on the carpet itself rather than on the sheets.

This couldn't be happening! What was she going to do? As soon as she had carefully folded the Noah's ark backdrop, she ran for the vacuum. It was just chalk dust. Surely it would vacuum up. She went over the entire carpet three times, but Noah's ark was still clearly visible.

She remembered there was some carpet cleaning shampoo under the kitchen sink. She sprayed a small area, grabbed a sponge, and began to scrub the carpet. This might have worked with a little spill, but Noah's ark covered the entire carpet. At this rate, it would take two weeks to clean up this mess—and the relatives were due back any minute!

At last, Julie gave up. Tears ran down her cheeks as she flopped down on the sofa, frustrated, angry at herself, and scared of facing her parents. After all, Mom had been saving for a long time to get the carpet professionally cleaned. What was she going to say now? Plus, Julie had embarrassed herself in front of her relatives. What would they think? Why, oh why, hadn't she paid attention to the voice in her head that had warned her that making the backdrop for the play on the living room carpet was not a good idea? If only she had listened! Because she ignored her conscience, she was now in big trouble. There was no way she could hide what she had done. Like it or not, she was just going to have to face the music. *Oh, this is not gonna be good. Mom will be furious!*

Before long, she heard the sound of the van pulling into the driveway. Julie ran out to warn her mom about the carpet, so she wouldn't explode at the sudden shock of seeing what Julie had done.

Waiting until she got close enough so the others wouldn't hear her, Julie whispered, "Mom, you won't believe what I've done. Wait 'till you see what's on the living room carpet."

"What's on the carpet?" Mom asked.

"*Ahhh*, Noah's ark!"

"Noah's ark?" her mother exclaimed. "What's it doing on the carpet?" Mom rushed up the steps and opened the front door—and screamed!

Dad was right behind her and, trying to lighten the mood, said, "Hey, I didn't know you were such a good artist!"

Everyone else had a good laugh at Julie's expense. However, Mom

wasn't laughing—and Julie wasn't either.

Two days later, the professional carpet cleaners came again. They said they had never cleaned the same carpet two times in one week—but appreciated the business. Julie, however, didn't appreciate it quite as much as they did, since the money she had been saving all year for summer camp paid the bill. ■

Do not cast me away from Your presence,
And do not take Your Holy Spirit from me.
—Psalm 51:11, NKJV

Tackling Tail Feathers

"Come on, you silly bird!" Cameron grabbed at the cockatiel, but only got a handful of air. "I can't get this one back in the cage."

"That's the one we just sold, right?" Cameron's mom came into the room and studied the baby cockatiel who was now as big as his parents.

"Yep. And the most stubborn one too." Cameron watched the bird fly in circles around the living room. "Why can't we clip its wings so it can't fly away?"

"That's a decision his new family will need to make. It won't be long, now, son. This bird will be gone by Christmas."

The Wilson family hadn't planned to raise cockatiels. Cameron had asked for a cockatiel the year before, hoping to get one that he could teach to talk. He had named the bird Adam.

Next year, Andy joined Adam. He was a cockatiel who had a feisty

personality, but the two birds soon became instant friends, preening each other and chirping back and forth.

Then one day, when Cameron went to feed the birds, the most unusual thing happened.

"Look what I found!" he hollered.

Mom peered inside the cage and exclaimed, "It's an egg!"

"It can't be. Only females produce eggs." Dad tried to ignore the commotion.

"Dad! It *is* an egg!" Cameron came closer and stared at the object Adam was rolling around. "He's trying to sit on it."

Cameron's dad cast a weary look their way, but soon joined his family. "It *IS* an egg!" He shook his head in disbelief.

"But how did those two birds have an egg?" Cameron asked.

"My guess is that Adam needs a new name since he is the one rolling around that egg. How about Eve?" His dad grinned.

Cameron looked at his birds. Maybe it was time to do some research on how to raise cockatiels.

It wasn't long before he had his answers. Females have a lighter cheek patch, and that was Adam, so he laid the egg, and that's how Adam became Eve! Andy was indeed the dad. Cameron made a soft, cotton nest for the egg and Eve and Andy took turns sitting on it. About three weeks later, to everyone's surprise, a really ugly baby bird hatched.

Eve and Andy were good parents. They spent long hours taking turns taking care of their new baby. It grew quickly and soon found a new home with Cameron's best friend. The miracle bird was given the name King Tut, and he went on to learn many words and musical phrases.

Now, the second clutch had been born, raised, and placed, all except the last bird which Cameron was trying to catch. A church family had bought the bird as a surprise Christmas present for their twins, but they didn't want to pick it up until right before the holiday. It was a beautiful bird, sleek with bright colored cheek patches. It had a mischievous personality and would be a perfect bird for two active children. What the new owners had admired most about the bird was its beautiful set of tail feathers that the cockatiel liked to fan out and preen.

Cameron grabbed at the bird again. "Hey bird, stop flying away! It's time to get back into your nice, clean cage." Nothing was working. Cameron often let the birds out to get some exercise. Getting them back into their cage, however, wasn't always so easy—as today was proving.

Cameron was getting impatient and his temper was getting the best of him. He knew he shouldn't be grabbing at the bird, but he was tired of this endless game!

Cameron watched as the bird landed on a laundry basket sitting on the floor. Maybe he had a chance now. He tried to sneak up on the bird, but he wasn't quick enough.

"I quit! I can't catch him!" Cameron plopped down on the couch.

"He's enjoying his freedom. Give him a minute to settle down and then try again." Cameron's mom had been watching the whole scene.

"I should have been at Tony's house thirty minutes ago! I need to get going now! I'll try one more time. Would you please help me, Mom?"

"I can try, but you know this is your job. You need to follow through with the care of the birds if you want the money when they are sold. Right?"

Photo taken by: cagraphicdesign.com

"Yeah, I guess. I just didn't know it was going to be this much work."

Cameron stood and placed himself behind the bird. He slowly reached over, putting his hand near the cockatiel. In one swift move, he grabbed the bird by its tail, which was something he knew he should never do! Immediately, the bird flew away . . . and in his hand Cameron held every one of the bird's beautiful tail feathers.

He stood there stunned in disbelief. What had he done now? What would the new owners think?

Mom looked at the feathers, then at the shock on Cameron's face. "Let's get him back in his cage, and then we'll figure out what to do next." Cameron's mom walked over to the bird and held her finger out. He compliantly hopped on. She took him over to his cage and he went right in. "I think he's in shock too," Mom chuckled.

"No kidding!" Cameron shook his head, not quite believing what he had just seen. He laid the tail feathers on the counter and stared at the bird in the cage. He looked terrible without his beautiful feathers. Going to Tony's was completely forgotten as Cameron tried to process what the consequences of his impatience were going to be.

"Will the feathers grow back? How long do you think it will take?" While Cameron was asking the questions, Mom was at the computer trying to find the answers.

"Hey, listen to this," Mom called to him. "Here's an article that says when cockatiels are frightened, they can drop their tail feathers as an escape mechanism for fleeing from their enemies. Isn't that amazing?"

"So, the bird was just doing what God created him to do?"

"Apparently so."

"I think it's cool that God created cockatiels with the ability to protect themselves. I guess I better call Mrs. Bailey and explain. Do you think she'll still want him?"

"If not," Mom replied, "you'll have to give the money back."

Cameron already had plans for the money he had earned by selling the babies. He didn't want to give it back, but he knew it would only be fair. He picked up the phone and dialed Mrs. Bailey's number.

A few minutes later, Cameron came into the kitchen where his mother was cleaning up. "What did she say?" Mom asked.

Cameron smiled, "She thought the whole thing was kind of funny. She still wants the bird." Cameron looked relieved. "She knows the feathers will grow back." He walked over to the cage and watched the rebellious bird stare back at him. "Without his tail feathers he looks like he hasn't gotten dressed yet." Cameron smiled.

"I guess today, son, you've learned a lesson about being patient. We have an amazing God, One that cares for all of His creatures, even rebellious birds," Mom responded.

Cameron grinned as he gave his mom a big hug. "The more I learn about God, the more I love Him." ■

> *Be joyful in hope, patient in affliction,*
> *faithful in prayer.*
> —Romans 12:12, NIV

Aunt Lucy's Cottage

"Mom, how long have you known Aunt Lucy?" Ellie looked across the lane to the quaint English cottage that stood all by itself in a garden full of beautiful flowers.

"Oh, ever since I can remember! She was best friends with your grandma. They used to walk to school together across the fields to Bramley. When they grew up, Grandma married Grandpa, and Aunt Lucy married Uncle Fred."

Ellie had never met Uncle Fred. He died just a few weeks before she was born. "What was Uncle Fred like?" asked Ellie.

"Well, he was kind and gentle and he knew everything about the flowers that grow in an English country garden! Aunt Lucy was a dressmaker back then. She made those lovely, little baby dresses for you that I keep in my memory chest.

"Since Aunt Lucy and Uncle Fred didn't have children of their own, they helped to look after my brothers and sisters and me, especially when your grandma was sick for a few months," Mom explained.

"Yes, and you took me to visit Aunt Lucy when I was only a tiny baby!" Aunt Lucy still had the photo of Ellie's first visit on her shelf.

Ellie loved Aunt Lucy, even though she wasn't her real aunt. Several times a week, Ellie would carefully cross the lane and walk through the flower garden to her country cottage. They would read stories, sew, bake cakes, or take her dog, Toby, for a walk. Aunt Lucy had a collection of china cottages, and one had a little roof that lifted off and there was space inside to hide a treat like a cookie or piece of candy. As Aunt Lucy grew older and found it harder to walk and move around, Ellie would run errands for her and play with Toby.

One day after breakfast, Ellie went to visit Aunt Lucy. She rang the front doorbell, but no one came. So she walked through the garden, knocked on the back door, and tried the handle. The door opened with a eerie *creeeeek*. She peeked into the room. There was Aunt Lucy lying on the floor! She was moaning with pain and looked cold and miserable. Toby sat beside her whimpering. His food and water bowls were licked completely clean.

Lucy picked up the phone and dialed home. "Mom, come quickly! Aunt Lucy's hurt! She needs help!"

She found a pillow and gently slid it under Aunt Lucy's head to make her more comfortable. Then she ran and got one of Aunt Lucy's homemade quilts and carefully covered her. Aunt Lucy smiled weakly. Ellie sat on the floor and held her hand, reassuring her that she would be OK.

It wasn't long before Mom came rushing in. "I've called the ambulance! They're on their way!" she announced. "Ellie, run outside and show the ambulance driver where to stop!"

Soon, Aunt Lucy was on her way to the hospital. It turned out she had a broken hip and it was going to take a long time to heal. She wasn't able to take care of herself, so she went to stay in a nursing home surrounded by pretty rose gardens that was located at the edge of the village. Toby went to stay with Ellie's family.

A few weeks later, Ellie celebrated her eleventh birthday. The day after her party, she took Aunt Lucy a piece of her birthday cake and a jar of bubbles. Mom carefully pushed Aunt Lucy's wheelchair into the garden. They blew bubbles together and laughed and giggled like old times. Back in her room, Aunt Lucy handed Ellie an envelope and a gift in a gold box, topped with a perfectly tied sparkly bow.

"What's this?" Ellie asked with a big smile on her face. She tore open the envelope and read, "To Ellie, the sweetest girl in the world. I love you very much. Happy Birthday! Aunt Lucy."

"Oh, thank you, Aunt Lucy! I love you too."

"Well, come on now, let's see what's inside the box. Be careful, though," Aunt Lucy said, "it's a bit fragile!"

Ellie carefully untied the ribbon and lifted the top off the box. Inside was lots of crumpled tissue paper, and inside the crumpled tissue paper was one of Aunt Lucy's china cottages. Ellie couldn't believe her eyes! This was her favorite cottage! The one that had a top like a box! The one Aunt Lucy hid treats inside!

Ellie squealed with delight! "Oh, thank you! Thank you!" she said excitedly as she jumped up and down. She hugged and kissed Aunt Lucy. Then a concerned look crossed her face.

"What's the matter? Don't you like it?" Aunt Lucy asked.

"Oh, yes, I love it. But . . . I can't possibly accept your gift. This is your very favorite cottage!"

"Well, it's your favorite one too, and I want you to have it. And don't forget to look inside. There just might be a treat waiting for you!" Aunt Lucy's eyes twinkled, waiting for Ellie's reaction.

Ellie wondered what it could be. Perhaps some candy, maybe a few coins, or a barrette for her hair? She quickly lifted the lid and placed it carefully on the table. Inside the china cottage was a piece of fabric left over from one of Ellie's baby dresses. And inside the fabric was something hard and oddly shaped. Ellie held the little fabric parcel in her hand and

gently unfolded it. Inside was the key to Aunt Lucy's front door.

Now Ellie was really confused. She knew her mom already had a key for the cottage. They used it when checking on the plants and looking after things.

Aunt Lucy saw the puzzled look on Ellie's face. "It's for you," she said with a smile. "I want to give my cottage to you."

Ellie picked up the china cottage. "Thank you!" she said again. "It's lovely, and I'll always treasure it."

Aunt Lucy smiled. "No, honey. I'm not sure you understand. Not just the china cottage. I mean my real house! You see, I don't have any family, and you've always been so kind to me. I couldn't love you more than if you were my real niece! I don't need my cottage anymore. It's much too big for me to live in — and too much work for me to take care of.

"Besides, I like living here now. I need nurses to look after me and I like the garden. I'm close to my friends."

Ellie looked puzzled.

"Don't worry! You won't live there right now. Your parents will rent it out and save all the money for you in the bank until you're all grown up and ready to live there yourself. But the cottage belongs to you. I couldn't think of a better way to show you how very much you mean to me and how much I love you! One day, I'm sure Jesus will reward you with a mansion in heaven. But, until then, my cottage is the best I can do!" ■

And now may the LORD show kindness and truth to you. I also will repay you this kindness, because you have done this thing.
—2 Samuel 2:6, NKJV